SALES MANAGEMENT
IN AN
EQUIPMENT DEALERSHIP

GEORGE M. KEEN

GEORGE M. KEEN
Wise Wolf Consulting, LLC

Printed Worldwide
First Printing 2024
First Edition 2024

ISBN: 979-8-9903024-0-2

10 9 8 7 6 5 4 3 2 1

SALES MANAGEMENT
IN AN
EQUIPMENT DEALERSHIP

Dedication

Let me start by dedicating this to the two people in my life who have always been my support over the last 53 years.

Over a span of 45 years in the professional realm, I've had the privilege of collaborating with an array of companies, clients, and manufacturers, each interaction enriching my journey. A special note of gratitude goes to Robert P. Currie, with whom I shared 15 memorable years of his 40 in the equipment dealer industry. His profound influence on my business philosophy cannot be overstated.

I extend my heartfelt appreciation to Ed McCoy, not just as my boss but as a dealer principal and friend across two industries, whose perspectives have offered me invaluable insights from an owner's standpoint. Additionally, working alongside Federico Lamas and Luther Hoy as sales managers was an exceptional opportunity to aid in structuring their strategies and teams.

To every dealer principal and sales manager, I've had the fortune to collaborate with over the last 45 years, your shared wisdom and fellowship have been instrumental to my growth.

And to you, the reader, embarking on this journey to redefine success in sales, this book is intended to be your companion as you strive to reach new heights. May it inspire you and guide you towards unparalleled achievements.

Book Reviews

I must say your book is an impressive piece of work. Your book stands out for its comprehensive approach, relevance, and depth. As someone who has delved into numerous sales books, I was particularly struck by how you managed to cover every aspect, from culture to compensation, in a unique and engaging manner.

As a sales manager, I can confidently say that your book is a valuable resource. It's the kind of 'playbook' that I would frequently consult for guidance and to keep my objectives in focus. I was pleasantly surprised to see that every note I made about potential additions or discussions was already covered in subsequent pages.

George, your book is more than just a guide. It's a blueprint for creating exceptional sales leaders. I thoroughly enjoyed reading it, and I'm grateful that you shared it with me. I hope you don't mind if I keep it as a reference for future use. Your work has left a lasting impression on me, and I'm sure it will do the same for many others.

Federico Lamas

Federico is the Sales Manager and Executive Vice President for Virginia Tractor, a John Deere Agricultural dealer in central Virginia with 6 locations and 20 equipment salespeople.

Congratulations on an excellent book! Wow, it's so in-depth and has so much "meat." A number of things that I really liked were:

The thoroughness of it. You cover so many bases that I can't imagine a single thing that's missing. If a sales manager were to read this book and apply the principles of it, what a superstar manager he/she would be! I can only imagine how incredible it would be to have a sales manager who even understood one-half of the points that you teach here. It's the bible for equipment sales managers.

But not just equipment sales managers…I like that you go into so many concepts that can be applied in any business. In fact, I want to re-read certain pages and discuss/implement the concepts with the managers in a couple of my businesses.

You've nailed it and included everything to ensure a sales manager's success

Excellent, excellent book, George. If there's anything I can do to help, please let me know!

Gary Wilson

Gary Wilson was a lift truck dealer principal. He has sold that business and diversified into a number of other industries. He also owns a company called MasterCheck.

Table of Contents

1. Introduction

What the Sales Manager is Responsible for Controlling

This book is about helping the sales manager understand their job and creating successful change in their company. Job descriptions for the sales manager are interesting. Still, significantly more needs to be understood about the market, the customers, the employees, and the sales manager's responsibilities.

To put it relatively simply, the sales manager is responsible for only three things: the sales activity, the quality of the sales calls, and the allocation of the effort.

Sales Activity

Sales activity can take various forms, including face-to-face, phone, and online interactions. The sales manager's responsibility is to optimize the outcomes across these diverse channels, ensuring successful sales achievements. Achieving this requires a keen understanding of optimal activity placement. This book will explore techniques for analyzing the market to identify the prime areas for business within your territory, encompassing your role, your company, and the broader industry.

Quality of Sales Calls

Achieving optimal results entails maximizing your efforts to the fullest extent. Subsequent chapters in this book will delve into key aspects, including the motivational factors driving sales professionals, the intricacies of the sales process structure, effective objection handling, and a comprehensive understanding of the various phases in customer purchasing.

Allocation of Effort

The market you operate in, the number of salespeople you currently have, the assets or financing you are allocated, and you and your staff's talents are just part of your resources.

Your choice of allocating these resources for maximum exposure and results is one of the primary responsibilities of the sales manager.

When you've achieved optimal sales activity, ensuring the highest possible quality, and strategically allocated resources for optimal coverage and impact, you set the stage for significant positive transformation within your department, your company, and your market.

Change Process

Management's job is sometimes so obvious that many people don't see what it is. It is simply to CHANGE BEHAVIOR!

Upon a closer examination of managerial expectations, it becomes evident that managers are responsible for influencing their employees' behavior. This influence aims to foster increased sales, heightened productivity, and a positive attitude. Managers are also tasked with steering customers' behavior towards increased purchases and increased satisfaction with the solutions offered by the company. One might even contemplate the role of managers in influencing the behavior of suppliers or vendors, aligning with the notion we just discussed regarding the transformative power of managerial behavior.

Elements of Successful Change

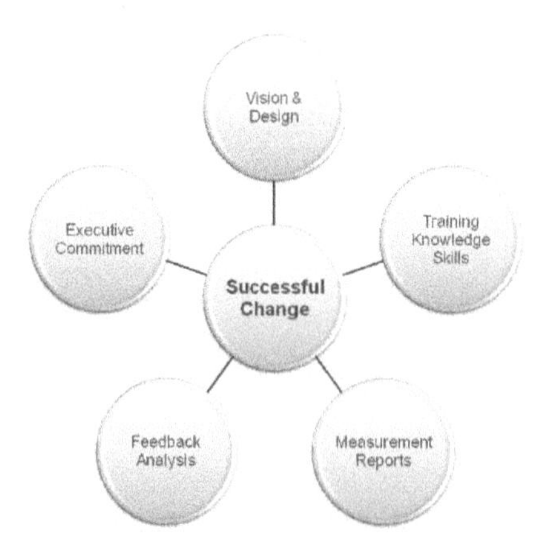

Successful change does not happen accidentally or without help. It takes work and effort, focus, and planning. Many business books have been written on this issue in the past. We see it coming down to five simple points, as illustrated in the diagram on this page.

Change that is accepted is also one that people feel they have some control over and involvement in. Change “thrust upon them” will seldom be appreciated and embraced.

Executive Commitment

The cornerstone of successful change lies in "Executive Commitment." Without this commitment from leadership, excuses and a lack of effort may permeate all levels involved. "Executive Commitment" goes beyond a mere speech to the team; it necessitates visibility, the allocation of resources, and diligent follow-through. True executive commitment entails active participation in meetings, the dedication of ample personnel, time, money, and resources, and a steadfast focus to drive the desired change.

Can we genuinely assert that an owner is committed to a cause if, post-meeting enthusiasm notwithstanding, they become preoccupied with other business matters and forget the initial excitement? We've encountered instances where clients' employees express sentiments like, "Give it a couple of weeks, and he'll return to his usual routine after attending one of those meetings." Where is the "Executive Commitment" in such a company?

Authentic executive commitment manifests in active participation during meetings, the strategic allocation of resources, and unwavering follow-through. We anticipate executives to invest not only in words but also in tangible commitments of money, time, personnel, and other resources for changes they genuinely endorse. At times, this may even involve reassigning projects to ensure individuals have the necessary time to fully dedicate themselves to the focal point of a change.

Vision/Design

When contemplating how to delineate a change, it proves beneficial to maintain clarity on two crucial aspects: firstly, identifying the benchmark for success in the particular issue or area, and secondly, establishing a method for gauging your present performance. To illustrate, consider aspiring to win a marathon. You're equipped with the knowledge of the race's distance and can analyze past race results to determine the winning time. These two components provide the metrics for success. Subsequently, measure your own time to cover the same distance. Your current performance is the baseline, while the race results are the benchmark for ultimate success.

Similarly, when embarking on a transformative journey in anything, defining the goal, envisioning the future, or outlining the blueprint for success is imperative. This could involve metrics like financial gains, speed, productivity, or other relevant factors. However, the absence of a clear benchmark for success leaves you without a yardstick to measure progress or achievement.

Training/Knowledge/Skills

After formulating and conveying a plan to the workforce, the focus shifts to cultivating the internal competencies necessary for executing the business plan. Without a well-defined plan, identifying gaps becomes elusive, hindering the development of the requisite skills. We must identify the gaps and implement training, development, and educational programs to help overcome the gaps. Additionally, there might be a need to assess whether the personnel required for plan execution are appropriately positioned.

Measurements/Reports

The next phase involves delivering suitable reinforcement to employees when they meet performance expectations. Here, we will briefly explore three types of reinforcement: positive reinforcement, negative reinforcement, and punishment. The table below outlines the characteristics of each.

The difference between negative reinforcement and punishment is often subtle and difficult to determine. Negative reinforcement, being seldom employed in management, lacks widespread applicability due to its general inappropriateness and the inherent complexities associated with its maintenance and subsequent enforcement. In contrast, punishment finds more prevalence in a business context. However, negative reinforcement and punishment exhibit limited efficacy with employees, as they tend to learn how to evade detection rather than address the undesirable behavior at its core.

Method	Definition	Example
Positive Reinforcement	Provides target with a positive stimulus when a desired behavior is displayed	Praising an employee after she does a good job on a project, report, etc.
Negative Reinforcement	Imposes an undesirable stimulus on the target until the undesired behavior ceases.	Withholding praise until an employee performs a task to your expectation (the lack of praise being the negative stimulus)
Punishment	Imposes an immediate and undesirable consequence in response to a specific behavior	Yelling at an employee who has performed a task poorly

Positive reinforcement proves significantly more effective and prevalent in managerial practices. It's simpler to acknowledge an employee for a job well done or to offer a bonus than resorting to the less constructive approach of giving the 'silent treatment.' However, a potential pitfall to navigate is the tendency to inundate employees with excessive positive reinforcement. Overwhelming praise can diminish its impact in eliciting the desired behavior. The crucial aspect lies in establishing a structured system where employees value the incentives provided, steering clear of saturation that might dilute the effectiveness of these incentives.

Analysis

If you have Executive Commitment, Vision, Training/New Knowledge, and Measurements, you still need to stop and analyze the process at various times. If you are not achieving success or the desired change, you must review the first four steps.

- Did you get "Executive Commitment" early but not get the follow-through?
- Were there adequate resources to accomplish the change?
- Was the direction, design, or vision clear and well communicated?
- Were these utilized after you did the training, shared the new knowledge, or provided the new skills?
- Were you measuring the correct variables to determine if you were making progress? Was there any outside influence on the benchmarks?

From analyzing these sorts of questions about your first four elements of successful change, you might gain greater insight into what is happening, why you are succeeding, and how to improve your progress toward the goal.

2. The Evolving Landscape

Crafting a market strategy is a dynamic process, a continuous effort that lays the groundwork for your company's triumph in a fiercely competitive environment. Managing sales and your department begins with understanding the evolution of the market around you. Regular market analysis, strategic planning, and effective management not only serve your customers efficiently but also pave the way for your company's sustained growth and profitability. Think of market strategy as the framework upon which you structure the future. The precision of your map becomes the linchpin of your success in reaching your desired destination.

The initial step in shaping any market strategy is delineating your market area - the geographic region where you will sell your products and services. Your Original Equipment Manager (OEM) may define your market area by establishing your Area of Responsibility (AOR). Whether your OEM or you set the market area, establishing too small a market area limits sales volume potential, while an excessively large one incurs higher servicing costs. Defining your market area as your "natural trading area," determined by time and travel routes rather than miles, helps with balance because neither your salespeople nor your technicians fly the same straight route as a bird. Rivers, highways, and other physical boundaries impact your natural trading area scope.

Zooming in on your market area pulls back the veil on untapped opportunities in equipment sales and aftermarket services. Delve into accounts not currently utilizing your services, including those handling their own service. Recognize that there might be accounts you're unaware of in your market area, suggesting abundant untapped potential.

The keys to success lie in concentrating efforts on a market area you can dominate, crafting strategies to assert that dominance, and executing tactics to make it a reality.

Once your market area is defined, the next crucial step is developing a strategy to target customers within that territory. The type of customers you engage with is pivotal to your business's success. Ideal customers are:

- profitable,
- growing,
- cost-conscious,
- making purchasing decisions to reduce cost instead of only to obtain a low initial price,
- prompt payers,
- companies that appreciate working with a focused group of suppliers and
- companies that understand the value of a long-term partnership.

Conversely, dealing with price-sensitive, unprofitable customers poses a challenge to your company's success. Do your very best to avoid it.

Given that the success of your business heavily depends on the kinds of customers you attract, it becomes evident that choosing the proper accounts is a pivotal aspect of your marketing strategy.

Approach targeting customers by focusing on two key categories:

Acquiring New Accounts: Tailor your strategies to attract new accounts that align with your business goals. Identify and reach out to potential new customers who resonate with your services. There is a natural attrition of customers who move, die, or find a cheaper competitor; therefore, Growing your customer base is essential for long-term success.

Optimizing Profits from Existing Accounts: Enhance your profitability by maximizing the potential of your current accounts. This involves cultivating solid relationships with your existing customer base and finding opportunities to provide additional value, ensuring they continue to benefit from your sales, service, consulting, and partnership.

Focusing on these two areas can drive sustained success for your total value package.

Before we dive below the surface of this core business strategy to the details, let’s learn about the evolving market. This will give us a framework for the rest of this chapter. The dynamics of the marketplace should drive your strategy.

Breaking down market evolution into four distinct phases, as shown in the chart, forms the framework for our strategic approach. Each phase is about innovation, or, put another way, there is continuous innovation.

Evolution of the Market

	Phase I	Phase II	Phase III	Phase IV
Marketing View of the World	Premium Product with a Premium Price	Premium Product with a Low Price	Premium Product with a Low Cost of Ownership	Premium Product with Low Cost of Process
Sales Process	**Product** Differentiation	**Price** Differentiation	**Total Cost of Ownership** Differentiation	**Total Cost of Process** Differentiation
Organization Structure	Geographic	Functional	Matrix	Process Centered
Offering	**Product**	**Product & Service**	**Lease with Maintenance**	**Rental**

In Phase I, the strategy revolves around product differentiation and distribution by direct sales, either by the manufacturer or a network of distributors in the customer's geographic area. The strategic approach in this phase revolves around product differentiation, and the distribution channels are centralized either through direct sales from the manufacturer or a distribution network structured around geographical considerations.

The manufacturer's objective is to establish an extensive network of dealers/distributors, covering a broad geographic scope to enhance visibility and market reach. Phase I marks the initial product entry into the market, setting the stage for Phase II, where competition intensifies as more players enter the market landscape.

Moving into Phase II, the landscape shifts as competitors enter the market, offering products comparable to yours. The competition knows what you charge for your products and services and offers a lower price point. They gain traction through aggressive pricing strategies, challenging the pioneer's market share. Intense marketing gives a savvy competitor an edge in capturing some of that market share from the established leader.

The interplay of marketing intensity and quality, both actual and perceived, directly influences market share. Lowering prices, a common market penetration strategy, proves effective sometimes, especially in mature markets. As competitors multiply and follow this cycle, the product evolves into a commodity, where price becomes the key differentiator. The Focus Issues portion of the PIMS study[1], for General Electric by Harvard, forms the basis for much of what we know about this subject.

The original player must reduce costs to lower the price point and stay competitive. This necessitates an organizational shift from a geocentric approach to a more functional approach. Dealers downsize certain functions and centralize others, with the salespeople reporting to a single sales manager, streamlining operations previously held by multiple autonomous departments or branches.

Despite its clear strategic advantages, Phase II is precarious. End users quickly recognize the competitive price warfare among rivals and leverage this knowledge to their advantage. In a bid to secure or retain business, dealers/distributors may resort to pricing at a loss, hoping to recoup in the aftermarket. The typical outcome involves a market shakeout, with some competitors consolidating or exiting the business. The remaining entities are divided between those capable of surviving as low-cost producers and those adapting to a Phase III mindset, successfully bringing end users along.

Phase III demands a higher level of expertise in a distributor's sales force. They must be able to help customers shift from Phase II to Phase III thinking, where the focus is still on price but also an openness to the idea that the cost to minimize extends beyond the acquisition cost to the total cost of product ownership. The dealer/customer relationship reaches Phase III when they adopt leasing with maintenance agreements, which consider upfront the costs associated with maintaining and repairing the equipment.

As dealers/distributors and manufacturers advance into Phase III, organizations typically shift from a functional structure to a more dynamic matrix structure. A matrix organization is a work structure where team members report to multiple leaders.

---

[1] Woo, C. Y., and Cooper, A. C. "Strategies for High Market-Share Companies." Harvard Business Review, November 1975. https://hbr.org/1975/11/strategies-for-high-market-sharecompanies.

In a matrix organization, team members (remote or in-house) report to a project manager and their department head. In Phase III, the traditional roles of manufacturer, dealer, and customer begin to morph into a holistic package of value-added activities, in which the same dealer provides the machine and the machine's parts and services, and the manufacturer is involved in the entire process. This integration of manufacturing, sales, and service enables the dealer/distributor to profit from all the customer's equipment needs.

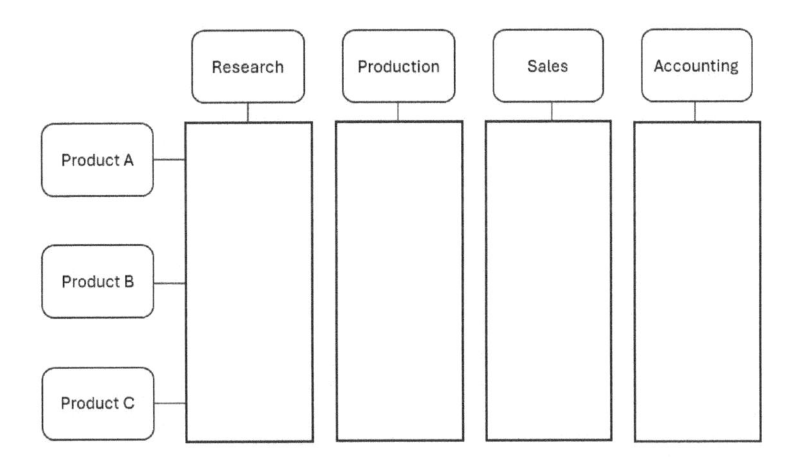

In Phase III, the organizational approach moves away from functional silos, shifting towards a cross-functional or matrix structure. While internally departments are still considered discretely for financial analysis, the dealer begins to package products and services based on the external view of the customer. This customer-centric approach reflects a strategic move to provide and profit from a seamless and integrated solution to meet all the client's equipment requirements from the outset.

Enter Phase IV, and customers no longer aim to purchase the product; instead, the dealer has convinced the customer it's in their best interest to integrate the product seamlessly into their entire business process. In Phase I, customers sought the best product; in Phase II, they aimed for the best product at the lowest price; in Phase III, their focus shifted to acquiring the best product with the lowest cost of ownership. Phase IV end users prioritize their core products and look to the dealer/distributor to handle the entire fleet management process.

In Phase IV, the dealer/distributor is a single provider for all the customer's equipment needs. The dealer essentially becomes another fixed cost for the customer based on usage metrics such as hour or miles. The pivotal shift in this phase lies in transforming the sales force from selling individual products like machinery and maintenance agreements to selling a more integrated value package.

As you can see, the distribution organization undergoes a profound shift towards becoming more process-centered in Phase IV. This distinguishing factor becomes the quality of service, emphasizing elements like minimal downtime and reliable maintenance. While price remains a consideration, quality takes precedence in the end user's supplier selection. Customers in Phase IV are willing to pay a premium for a premium process.

Dealers/distributors must be able to serve a diverse group of customers, recognizing that they have customers in each phase discussed above. The reality is that the most effective salesman for Phase I or Phase II may not be as effective in selling to Phase IV customers. This necessitates organizational transformation to adequately meet customers' needs in each phase, formulating strategies for customer service that integrate market share, quality, and marketing intensity into the action plan, focusing on maximizing return on assets.

Understanding the Evolution of the Market serves as the foundation for our focus on key issues and the Financial Model. The strategies outlined here are crafted to ensure our ability to serve all four phases and to build robust systems and processes that enhance organizational capabilities and profits. The entire organization must embrace the understanding that being one-dimensional is not an option; success requires active engagement across all four phases.

Related Sales Strategies

Adapting to market evolution starts with your salespeople understanding their customers' myriad motivations, influences, and purchasing decision motivations. A crucial aspect is recognizing how individuals transition in purchasing decisions as they encounter different product categories and innovations within an industry.

Some customers shift, over time, from old purchasing patterns to embracing innovation and change.

A successful sales strategy involves understanding and facilitating that evolution by understanding factors that motivate your customers to buy what you're selling.

Product, Brand & Dealership

The surge of choices is overwhelming in an increasingly crowded marketplace characterized by continuous manufacturing, distribution, and communications advancements. The phenomenon known as "product convergence" has made it challenging for companies to distinguish their products amidst the flood of new offerings. The prevailing wisdom for success lies in strategically marketing your brand, not just the product itself.

Certain customers strongly identify with brands, a sought-after connection for most manufacturers. Some even desire to have their brand integrated into your company name, envisioning local dealers or distributors as extensions of their marketing endeavors. This arrangement proves advantageous when exclusively representing a single brand, unwavering in allegiance, and never considering other products or brands.

Consider the scenario of representing a powerhouse brand like McDonald's Restaurants, boasting one of the strongest global brand recognitions in the restaurant industry. While this affiliation brings substantial value, it comes with a trade-off – adherence to numerous regulations, rules, and promotions that can impact various aspects of your business, including profitability, operating hours, and hiring practices. Opting for a robust or exclusive focus on a brand name has both positive and negative implications that demand careful evaluation.

Crucially, some customers prioritize a product based on the brand itself, often with little concern for the price. In sales and marketing, your primary objective is to sell, and understanding and accommodating the customer's preference for a particular brand is a vital aspect of success. Ignoring this aspect could mean overlooking a significant factor influencing the customer's buying decision.

Price

"Take Wal-Mart, and price is their game-PERIOD! They have wiped out many small companies—Also Costco, Sam's Club, etc. I rest my case: PRICE IS KING, no matter how you slice and dice your crafty articles. Risk, value, and any other sales gimmicks don't make it."

While common among salespeople and even competitors, the sentiment expressed may overlook the intricate strategy behind how Walmart maximizes its profitability. Walmart strategically designates 850-2,000 highly price-sensitive items and possibly 200 additional local items as "Everyday Low Prices." However, it's crucial to note that the typical Walmart store carries a vast inventory of around 120,000 stock-keeping units (SKUs). This means the majority—118,000 items—were not designated as "Everyday Low Priced." That was a solid element of Walmart's strategy for years. In the past decade, Walmart has gone beyond "everyday Low Prices" to broadening its assortment of stocked items by 11% in most brick-and-mortar locations, adding "price matching," "Rollback Pricing," and leveraging technologies. Walmart has reduced costs and remained competitive in a growing digital marketplace while offering low prices.

When a salesperson insists on being the lowest price on a quotation, it often translates to a desire to avoid handling price objections. Price is a more straightforward element to address in a sale compared to selling on factors like value, quality, service, or delivery.

Customers and prospects will undoubtedly express concerns about price, and some may explicitly seek the lowest price. However, it's crucial to recognize that not every customer is solely driven by the lowest cost. While some are meticulous about prices and features, they may not represent the entire market. It's important to distinguish the more vocal contacts from the broader customer base.

A current perspective suggests that customers truly seek to lower their risk in a transaction. While cost reduction mitigates risk, fostering a better relationship between the salesperson and the buyer also reduces risk. Effectively addressing concerns beyond the "lowest cost" provides avenues to minimize potential issues in various situations.

Total Cost of Ownership

Total Cost of Ownership (TCO) is a comprehensive financial estimate crucial for consumers and enterprise managers across various industries. Essentially a form of full cost accounting, TCO considers direct and indirect costs associated with a particular asset or investment. It aims to provide a holistic understanding to customers of the impact of their purchase, encompassing factors like initial cost, delivery, maintenance, fuel economy, and residual value.

An illustrative example from one company's past involves analyzing the best company car for a Swiss firm. Despite evaluating various European brands such as Renault, Fiat, Citron, and Ford, the seemingly expensive Mercedes Benz was the recommendation. This decision was grounded in economic rationale, considering factors like initial purchase price, fuel costs, fuel economy, and the car's retained value. In the long run, the Mercedes Benz proved to hold its value better than any other competitive brand.

It's worth noting that the analysis did not capture potential savings in vehicle downtime or improvements in employee productivity. If the chosen product not only incurs lower maintenance costs but also demands less frequent maintenance, the actual savings for the buyer could surpass the illustrated figures.

In essence, TCO guides buyers towards a more informed decision-making process, emphasizing the long-term economic benefits rather than fixating on the initial purchase price. This approach ensures a more comprehensive evaluation, considering the broader financial implications and potential operational efficiencies.

Fleet Management &/or Outsourcing

Outsourcing equipment management and all associated services and information has become a prevalent strategy for fleets. This strategic shift allows fleets to concentrate on their primary competency—efficiently moving goods and meeting customer demands.

In the current business landscape, outsourcing stands out as one of the most significant global trends. Unlike when companies invested substantial resources attempting to be self-sufficient across various functions, the prevailing realization is that dealerships should prioritize their core activities. Instead of trying to handle everything internally, companies are recognizing the value of establishing interdependent relationships with top-tier providers for processes and systems that fall outside their core competencies. This shift allows them to leverage the expertise of specialized partners and enhances their overall operational efficiency.

GE offers a seminar to potential clients. "This is part of our sales process," says Steve Greenway, strategic consultant for Minneapolis-based GE Commercial Finance Fleet Services. "It's not really a matter of who has the cheapest truck to offer-it also involves things like how to get the vehicles licensed and to your location and then how to get rid of the old trucks."

The one-day seminar is designed to help everyone involved in these decisions, including fleet management personnel, the CFO, treasurer and the tax director.

The responsibilities of today's fleet manager are far different and more complex than those of predecessor managers. "Years ago, the fleet manager ordered pretty much whatever fleet vehicles he wanted to," Lefever says. "But with the bad economy and tight money, fleet managers now work closely with corporate finance people and risk managers in deciding which vehicles will be acquired and how long they will be kept."

Today's fleet managers tend to be less involved in the smaller day-to-day activities if they are outsourcing some components of management. Says Greenway: "They are involved more with the strategic direction of the fleet and they still need to make some of the high-level decisions like what kinds of vehicles they will need."

Historically, the focus of fleet management was on asset management, says Paul Lauria, president of Gaithersburg, Maryland-based Mercury Associates, Inc., a fleet management firm. "This means the acquisition, care, upkeep, replacement and disposal of vehicles and equipment," he says. Fleet managers are still expected to understand how to buy the right types of vehicles and how to acquire them at a good price, how to get them maintained and repaired and when to replace them. "These things are all in the price of admission," Lauria continues. "But fleet managers have to think like business managers. They are fleet regulators rather than providers of services to fleet users. This implies a much more collaborative posture, which is more customer-service oriented."[2]

As intelligent buyers become well-versed in the Total Cost of Ownership (TCO) concept, questions may arise within a company about the necessity of "owning these units." While understanding the TCO provides valuable insights, it doesn't eliminate the need for someone, typically the fleet manager, to handle the intricacies of purchasing, maintenance, downtime management, and unit replacement. At a certain point, a critical question emerges: Does this operational aspect truly create value for our organization?

This introspection often leads to considering outsourcing the function to external entities, and companies like yours could be positioned as potential outsourcing partners.

In an outsourcing arrangement, an organization assumes the risks and takes on the complete spectrum of functions related to fleet management. This comprehensive service comes at a fee, reflecting the risks of managing the assets' investment.

For the customer, outsourcing can offer significant advantages. It involves transferring the risks and responsibilities of fleet management to a specialized organization, freeing up capital

[2] Steve Greenway (now retired) was the Architect for GE Capital's suite of Excel-based financial analysis and sales tools for almost 27 years. This quotation is from an article in World Trade magazine.

investment and minimizing distractions from their core functions. While there is a cost associated with outsourcing, the potential benefits, including enhanced focus on core competencies and reduced operational burden, can often outweigh the financial considerations. It's a strategic shift that aligns with the evolving trend of companies recognizing the value of concentrating on their core business while entrusting specialized functions to external partners.

Package of Value

The typical distribution network vision is defined as follows: "To effectively market and serve a 'Package of Value' to specific end users while maintaining or exceeding benchmark financial performance." Let's break down this vision statement and explore the requirements to fulfill it.

Each dealer/distributor and manufacturer possess a unique "package" that should be marketed to its customer base. This package includes product sales, parts, service, and rentals. The goal is to sell all these elements to every customer. Traditionally, equipment is sold outright, with service contracts offered as additional services. There's a growing trend toward leasing machines and bundling a service agreement with the lease. The future expectation is that customers will request a comprehensive package that includes equipment, maintenance, parts, and rental units at a unified price.

When these product and service offerings are sold as a package, it effectively secures 100% of the end user's business. The advantages are manifold: a decisive advantage in unit replacements, control over all service labor for maintenance and repairs, capture of all parts business, and a higher likelihood of gaining service work and parts business for competitive units, potentially leading to the replacement of these units with the main product line.

The landscape of industrial selling is evolving with new ideas and practices such as benchmarking, reengineering, alliances, empowerment, total quality, micromarketing, relationship marketing, and downsizing.

These changes impact industrial selling from the perspectives of customers, competitors, and the salesperson's company. Adapting to this evolving environment requires careful monitoring of market changes, understanding customer needs, and adjusting selling strategies accordingly.

Success hinges on serving customers' needs better than anyone else and being appropriately compensated for the value provided. While outstanding products and services are crucial, true success comes from building a package that addresses customers' actual needs, offers genuine value, and sets your company apart from the competition.

Creating Packages of Value may involve collaborations within the dealership/distributor – manufacturer relationship. Some packages may be beyond individual capabilities and may require cooperation within this relationship. The Financial Model guides in determining the profit potential of any Package of Value.

Customers seek the optimal Package of Value, carefully analyzing various options based on what is crucial for their success. To sell more, your prospects must perceive your Package of Value as distinct and superior to competitors' offerings. This emphasis on delivering unique value becomes the driving force for customers to choose your package over alternatives, ultimately contributing to your success in the market.

1. Product:

The primary product sold is the equipment, the cornerstone of traditional sales for dealers and distributors over the years.

2. Services:

As the equipment market becomes saturated or reaches a point of normalcy, the sales focus often shifts to follow-on products, specifically services and replacement parts. These items are often more consumable than the equipment itself and can yield higher profit margins. Additionally, considering that customers in the second phase of market evolution are seeking more price reductions on equipment, services, and replacement parts, they become critical components of the sales strategy.

3. Information:

In the third phase of market evolution, customers start emphasizing the total cost of ownership. Analyzing this cost requires a wealth of information, more comprehensive than in earlier purchasing phases. Dealerships/distributors and salespeople assume a new role, evolving into consultants to their customers. Gathering relevant information, understanding the necessary data, and elucidating the impact of this new information on costs and purchasing decisions become the value that salespeople bring to the transaction. It's no longer just about product knowledge or price negotiation; it's about providing valuable insights through meaningful data.

4. Programs:

Programs are designed to assist customers or prospects transitioning to the next buying phase. These individuals seek a combination of product, price, and information bundled together in a program. While some may perceive this as "fleet management," it extends beyond merely managing a fleet of equipment. Programs offer a holistic approach, addressing the varied needs of customers in a comprehensive and organized manner.

Research & Results on Market Segmentation

% of World GDP	GDP in US $	# of Countries	% of Countries	% of Population	Population
43.00%	$43,425,900M	2	1.13%	22.8%	1,764M
29.05%	$29,193,460M	11	6.21%	29.6%	2,292M
19.95%	$20,078,752M	34	19.21%	26.8%	2,075M
8.00%	$6,226,812M	130	73.45%	20.7%	1,602M
100.00%	**$98,924,924M**	**177**	**100.00%**	**100.0%**	**7,733M**

Pareto's Rule 80/20:

The Pareto Principle, commonly known as the 80-20 rule, asserts that roughly 80% of effects result from 20% of causes. Originating from the observations of Italian economist Vilfredo Pareto on income and wealth distribution in Italy, this principle has been applied to various aspects of life. For instance, in terms of world GDP distribution, the top 23% of the population holds 43% of income, showcasing a significant imbalance. The principle has been used to explain economic inequality, but critics argue against its application in specific contexts, such as income distribution in the USA. That is not our issue here. We want to recognize that this approach helps identify the most significant volume of potential business for your dealership/distributor.

Original Research A-B-C-D

Wise Wolf Consulting, Inc. conducted original research over 30 years ago, refining the 80/20 principle to better understand the balance of business relative to the number of accounts.

Instead of a broad 80/20 split, we categorized business history into four segments: 40%, 30%, 20%, and 10%. This approach provided a more detailed perspective on customer relationships.

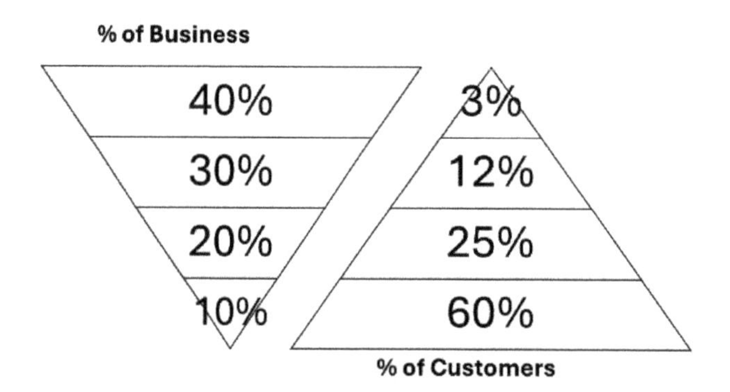

With modern computer systems and accessible spreadsheet interfaces, clients can quickly analyze their sales history. The process involves organizing customer sales data in a spreadsheet, sorting it from largest to smallest, and then examining running totals to identify breaks at the 40%, 30%, 20%, and 10% thresholds. This segmentation allows for a more nuanced understanding of where the majority of business is concentrated.

A crucial cautionary note is given to clients regarding the potential limitations of using a single year of data. Large capital purchases in one year may distort the analysis if not considered over a more extended period. Wise Wolf Consulting recommends utilizing a five to seven-year history to account for such cyclical patterns, capturing the full spectrum of customer activities, including equipment purchases and subsequent service or warranty-related transactions. This comprehensive historical perspective enables a more accurate and insightful segmentation analysis.

Recent Studies of Dealers in Multiple Industries

Despite the significant value derived from the research conducted over the past 30 years, Wise Wolf Consulting, LLC. recognizes the need for periodic reviews and updates.

The evolving landscape of the business environment has brought about notable shifts, particularly in the size and consolidation of large accounts.

Observations indicate that large accounts are growing and expanding through acquisitions. The sheer size of these accounts often results in the elimination of smaller competitors that once coexisted. Consequently, the distribution of accounts across the previously established categories (A-B-C-D) is changing, reflecting the market's dynamic nature.

This ongoing review and update process allows Wise Wolf Consulting and its clients to adapt to the evolving business scenario, ensuring that segmentation strategies remain accurate and relevant. By staying attuned to the shifting dynamics, dealerships can optimize their sales activities for maximum impact in the ever-changing market environment.

Segment	Dealer #4	Dealer #1	Dealer #8	Dealer #2	Dealer #3	Dealer #5	Dealer #6	Dealer #7	Dealer #9	% of Accounts
A	0.74%	0.76%	0.94%	0.96%	1.51%	1.53%	1.63%	2.30%	4.81%	**1.30%**
B	2.85%	3.00%	4.57%	3.68%	4.80%	5.27%	6.77%	6.33%	14.00%	**4.70%**
C	7.68%	9.31%	14.01%	11.64%	9.76%	14.60%	16.38%	12.29%	29.54%	**12.37%**
D	34.77%	86.93%	80.48%	83.72%	83.92%	78.60%	75.22%	79.09%	51.64%	**81.63%**
Total	100.00%	100.00%	100.00%	100.00%	100.00%	100.00%	100.00%	100.00%	100.00%	**100.00%**

Observations on Account Distribution:

While variations exist among companies regarding the percentage of accounts contributing to the top 40%, 30%, or each category, a noteworthy trend is the changing landscape revealed by the research and historical data. The adage "the rich get richer, and the poor get poorer" finds resonance in the business context, suggesting that large accounts increasingly constitute a more significant portion of revenue and market share in various industries. Conversely, smaller accounts are representing a diminishing share compared to the past.

This evolving pattern underscores the importance of regularly revisiting and updating market segmentation research. The dynamics of the business environment are in constant flux, and dealerships must adapt their strategies to reflect these changes. Analyzing sales history through the lens of this research provides valuable insights into the primary drivers of business activity.

It is a strategic tool for dealerships to align their efforts with the evolving landscape, ensuring they focus on the segments that contribute most significantly to their success in the current market conditions.

Illustrations of Multiple Industries

	Lift Truck	Agricultural	Construction	Commercial Tires	Transport Refrigeration	Heavy Trucks
Row Labels	% of Accts	% of Accts	% of Accts	% of Accts	% of Accts	% of Accts
A	1.51%	1.36%	1.53%	2.30%	4.81%	0.39%
B	4.80%	3.24%	5.27%	6.33%	14.00%	1.26%
C	9.76%	11.09%	14.60%	12.29%	29.54%	253%
D	83.92%	85.66%	78.60%	79.09%	51.64%	95.82%
Grand Total	100.00%	100.00%	100.00%	100.00%	100.00%	100.00%

Consistency Across Industries:

Indeed, every industry has its unique history, levels of consolidation, and dynamics at the top. However, the sample of clients across various sectors presented here illustrates the fundamental consistency of the analysis. The pattern of large accounts dominating the top, while smaller accounts occupy the bottom, holds true regardless of the industry or the stage of market evolution.

This cross-industry consistency highlights the universal applicability of the segmentation analysis. Whether in a mature industry or one undergoing evolution, the fundamental principles of account distribution remain robust. It emphasizes the enduring nature of particular market dynamics that transcend industry-specific nuances.

As dealerships navigate the complexities of their respective industries, understanding and leveraging these consistent patterns can provide a solid foundation for strategic decision-making. The insights derived from this analysis contribute to a more informed and adaptable approach, allowing dealerships to optimize their sales strategies in alignment with the prevailing market conditions, irrespective of industry specifics.

Examining the Relationship Between Customer/Accounts and Business Volume:

In evaluating the inverse relationship between the number of customers/accounts and the volume of business, it's crucial to explore whether this principle universally applies. By scrutinizing the first four left columns of the chart, the accounts were grouped based on their volume of business. The analysis involved counting the accounts and determining the percentage of accounts required to achieve the top 40%, the subsequent 30%, and so forth.

This granular examination allows for a nuanced understanding of how business volume correlates with the distribution of accounts. It provides insights into the concentration of revenue within specific account segments. While the inverse relationship is a prevalent trend, conducting this detailed analysis helps to validate its applicability in different scenarios.

This data-driven approach aids dealerships in refining their strategies and recognizing patterns specific to their industry or market evolution stage. It offers a more comprehensive view of the interplay between the number of accounts and the corresponding business volume, facilitating informed decision-making and strategic planning tailored to the unique characteristics of each business context.

Row Labels	# of Accts	% of Accts	% of Total $	% of Equip $	% of Rental$	% of Parts$	% of Service$
A	83	1.51%	39.82%	41.52%	52.86%	28.84%	38.52%
B	263	4.80%	30.17%	32.11%	20.60%	36.68%	28.26%
C	535	9.76%	20.01%	22.53%	18.76%	19.11%	17.95%
D	4598	83.92%	10.00%	3.84%	7.78%	15.37%	15.26%
Grand Total	5479	100.00%	100.00%	100.00%	100.00%	100.00%	100.00%

Analyzing Equipment Sales Across Account Segments:

Examining equipment sales within a dealer's business provides valuable insights into the distribution of sales volume across different account segments. In this specific case, the "A Accounts" represented a substantial 42% of the sales, indicating a strong correlation between higher account ranking and sales volume. On the contrary, the "D Accounts" contributed only 4% to equipment sales, emphasizing a clear hierarchy in purchasing behavior.

Further exploration into rental sales reinforces this trend, with 53% of rental sales originating from the "A Accounts" and a mere 8% from the "D Accounts." This underscores customers' preferences and purchasing patterns across various account segments, particularly in the equipment and rental categories.

However, a different dynamic emerges when delving into parts and service categories. These categories exhibit a more balanced distribution, with less than 40% of their volume coming from the "A Accounts" and approximately 15% from the "D Accounts". Recognizing the variability in customer behavior across different product categories is essential.

The critical takeaway lies in the accounts' holistic perspective of total business. While there may be variations in the sales mix based on product categories, the focus should be on the overall value of the total accounts. The goal is to capture all aspects of business from the accounts that constitute the top 40% of sales, irrespective of the specific product category. This approach aligns with a comprehensive business strategy that goes beyond merely selling equipment, emphasizing the broader spectrum of products and services offered by the company.

Illustration of Segmentation on A/R Aging

Strategic Insights from Accounts Receivable Analysis:

In this unconventional approach to Accounts Receivable (A/R) organization, segmentation based on previous purchasing volume provides unique insights. The accounts were then aged, following the standard "Current," "Over 30," "Over 60," and "Over 90" categories. Surprisingly, the "A Accounts" not only fit into the expected ratio grid but showed favorable performance in the "Over 60" and "Over 90" categories, suggesting they are diligent in settling bills. Conversely, the challenge lies with "D Accounts," which exhibit discrepancies in adhering to payment terms despite constituting only 10% of standard purchasing.

Benchmark Aging for Receivables in Many Industries:

Benchmark·Aging·for·Receivables·in·many·Industries¤			
Current¤	Over·30¤	Over·60¤	Over·90¤
70%¤	15%¤	10%¤	5%¤

Analyzing the aging column percentages for the “D Accounts” reveals a notable deviation from expected values, with higher percentages in each category. Despite their smaller transaction sizes and longstanding relationships, these accounts represent only 10% of all purchasing but hold over 30% of outstanding cash.

Looking at the aging in the company’s open A/R table above, we notice that the “B Accounts” and “C Accounts” fit into this expected ratio grid and beat it very nicely. The “A Accounts” are a little heavier in the “Over 30” category but are not as heavy as we might expect in the “Over 60” and “Over 90” categories, leading us to believe that they also are not bad at paying their bills. So, if “A Accounts” are not too bad, and the “B & C” accounts are better than the benchmark, what causes the problem at the bottom line? Of course, as our terms are laid out, the “D Accounts” are not paying their bills, and our expectations would project.

D Account % of Each Aging Column			
Current	Over 30	Over 60	Over 90
25.76%	39.93%	42.54%	58.47%

The question arises: Why should the “D Accounts” receive special treatment, delaying payments and affecting cash flow? Often, sentiment and historical relationships cloud the judgment, but when viewed objectively, they contribute disproportionately to outstanding cash.

Why should the “D Accounts” be allowed to drag their feet, keep the dealer's or distributor's cash, and get special treatment? Generally, the issue is that there are many small transactions, each one has a story or has been a friend for a long time. But these accounts only represent 10% of all the purchasing in this company, and besides being maybe 60% of all the customer accounts for the dealer who only do the last 10% of sales, they also hold 30%+ of all the outstanding cash.

Maybe someone needs to look at business areas like Accounts Receivable, Credit Management, Sales Efforts, and many other things differently. This discussion of A/R Aging is only a tiny illustration of some things you might want to look at differently when you begin segmenting your accounts.

This scenario prompts reevaluating business areas such as Accounts Receivable, Credit Management, and Sales Efforts. The A/R aging analysis is a small illustration of potential areas to scrutinize differently when implementing account segmentation. By reassessing the treatment of accounts based on their contribution to overall business and financial health, companies can optimize their strategies for improved efficiency and cash flow management.

Strategic Approach to Segmentation: Focusing on Profitable Growth

In crafting a segmentation strategy, deciding whether to target large or small accounts or maintain the status quo is pivotal and carries profound implications for your business. This choice stands out as the linchpin, holding more sway over your business trajectory than any other decision you might make.

The linchpin concept centers on the understanding that achieving high customer share among the largest accounts inherently translates into high market share and lays the core of profit potential. The philosophy is simple: aim for substantial customer share among large accounts to unlock profitability.

However, a nuanced approach is necessary. Not all large accounts are created equal. Each demands a discerning analysis to identify the ones that align with your business goals. Some may prioritize price over value, while others might pose financial risks or display a reluctance to pay on time. It's crucial to meticulously assess each potential large account to ensure a strategic fit.

The fishing analogy aptly captures the essence of this strategy. Why cast a wide net when the big fish are concentrated in a specific area? Opting to target the 30% of accounts responsible for 90% of business in your market zone is a pragmatic move. It's about maximizing profitability and sales volume by focusing efforts where they yield the most significant returns.

Conversely, dealing with numerous smaller accounts proves less profitable, demanding disproportionate time and resources for service. These accounts often come with elevated financial risks and offer limited sales volume and profitability potential.

In summary, your analysis of customer selection should guide you toward a clear conclusion: target accounts that promise high sales volume and significant profit opportunities. By aligning strategic choices with this principle, you position your business for growth, efficiency, and sustained profitability.

3. Fundamental Business Strategy

Market Analysis

Market analysis is a pivotal starting point for any strategic business initiative, especially in the realm of industrial equipment sales. Understanding the market landscape provides a solid foundation for effective decision-making. We could actually start practically anywhere on this process chart, but we'll start with the market analysis.

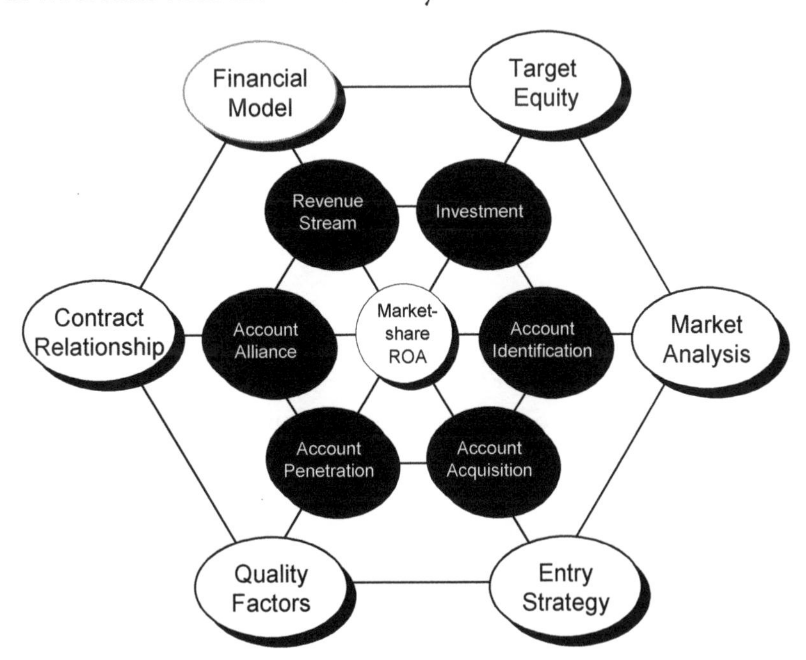

Working from the various phases of the market evolution, we can organize our known customers (and possibly our prospects) into what we believe their buying phase is. It might even be easier to start with an assumption that everyone is in Phase II. Then begin asking questions about some of your larger accounts:

1. Is the customer inclined towards making extended commitments?
2. Does the customer perceive our product/service as a unified system?
3. Does the customer view this acquisition as intricate or straightforward?
4. Are we considered a competitive supplier or a provider of an integrated system?

5. Is the customer already familiar with our product?
6. Does the customer perceive this purchase as a significant risk?

If you start answering these questions from the customer's perspective, you might decide they are not a Phase II buyer, but a Phase III or IV buyer. That could change your entire approach to the account. That realization could impact your approach or even the assignment of a salesperson.

Evolution of the Market:

Markets are dynamic, and comprehending their evolution is essential for strategic planning. This involves understanding how the demand for industrial equipment, including machines, parts, and services, has evolved over time. Consider factors such as technological advancements, changing customer needs, and industry trends.

Doing a Market Analysis:

Performing a comprehensive market analysis is a strategic move. Here's a breakdown of what it entails:

1. Territory Overview: Identify the key players in your target territory. This includes not only competitors but also potential collaborators or clients. Map out the competitive landscape to understand your position in the market.

2. Territory: for your dealership AOR may be specified by the manufacturer. But you need to. Carve out groups of territories for salespeople based on Potential, Capability, and Talent. Remember, a strong correlation exists between the number of pieces of equipment a prospect owns and their potential revenue value. We're going to dig into that process later in the book.

3. Potential and Phases: Assess the potential for your services, including machines, parts, and service. Analyze the current demand and project future trends. Understanding the different phases of market evolution helps tailor your approach. For instance, in a rapidly evolving market, there might be more emphasis on innovation and adaptability. Assess your own strengths and weaknesses. Are you good at moving equipment with low handling costs, or do you have the talent in your staff to deliver total Fleet Management in a Phase IV market? Knowing your strengths and weaknesses will assist you in focusing on your long-term strategy.

Characteristics of Dealerships

Dealer Performance Levels

High Performers

- Effective Sales Management Strategies
- Mentorship and skill development
- Well-defined goals for sales and profits
- Consistent meetings to discuss sales progress
- Yearly planning for sales and setting budget guidelines
- Allocation of specific customer accounts to sales team members
- Emphasis on both the quantity and quality of product support
- Maintaining a diverse range of sales, encompassing parts, services, and rentals.
- Holistic approach to client accounts, avoiding isolated department-focused sales efforts

Average Performers

- Conventional methods of sales territory coverage
- Modest performance expectations
- Irregular scheduling of sales meetings
- A mix of skilled salespeople and tolerance for underperformers
- Typically assigned sales regions
- Influenced by the most vocal complaints from sales staff
- Facing issues of compartmentalized management within the dealership

Low Performers

- Minimal to Absent Management
- Lack of a structured training program
- No defined goals or performance benchmarks
- Extensive territories assigned to sales staff
- Relying primarily on the compensation plan to motivate salespeople
- Treating service aspects as an unwelcome requirement within the dealership
- Virtually no defined career progression opportunities for employees

4. Account Identification: Consider account identification once you have a clear market picture. This involves identifying potential clients who align with your services. Consider their needs, preferences, and the phase of market evolution they are in. This targeted approach enhances the efficiency of your client acquisition efforts. Later, we'll discuss account priority, call frequency, and building relationships.

1. Client Segmentation: Segment potential clients based on their needs and the required services. This segmentation allows for a more personalized and effective approach.

2. Value Proposition: Develop a compelling value proposition highlighting your dealership's unique benefits. What sets you apart in terms of expertise, reliability, or cost-effectiveness?

3. Engagement Strategy: Craft an engagement strategy that aligns with the identified market phases. This could involve tailored marketing campaigns, outreach initiatives, or strategic partnerships.

4. Continuous Monitoring: Market dynamics are ever-changing. Implement a system for continuous monitoring and adaptation. Regularly revisit your market analysis to stay ahead of trends and proactively adjust your strategies.

Remember, this is an iterative process. As the market evolves, so should your approach. If you have specific questions or if there's a particular aspect you'd like to dive deeper into, feel free to let me know. Your proactive stance in understanding and navigating the market sets a solid foundation for building and expanding your client base.

Entry Strategy

Your strategic insight into the nuanced approach required for different market phases is crucial. Tailoring your strategy to each customer segment's specific needs and maturity demonstrates a keen understanding of the market dynamics. Let's explore the key points further:

In the realm of traditional approaches, one common strategy involves assigning territories. This implies that salespeople prioritize all accounts within their designated region. The assumption is that salespeople are familiar with all accounts in their territory and will proactively reach out to them.

However, as the market dynamics evolve, a more effective approach might be to assign specific accounts to salespeople. Implementing this approach efficiently may necessitate the use of a CRM system.

Many years ago, a sales manager related his early career to me. He graduated college and got a sales job. The dealership assigned him a territory. He WOW'd them with his performance! So, they cut his territory in half! He WOW'd them again the second year, and they cut his territory in half AGAIN! What was happening was that neither he nor the dealership understood the potential in that geography! The underlying issue was a lack of understanding, both on the part of the salesperson and the dealership, regarding the untapped potential within that geographical area. A more insightful approach would have involved assigning a smaller geography or a specific group of accounts based on their potential.

Bringing up the Pareto Principle and further categorizing accounts into A-B-C-D tiers can significantly impact the management of your sales team. This segmentation isn't a short-term strategy but rather a result of a more extended 5 to 8-year analysis. Once achieved, you may consider developing specialized teams or salespeople for A and B accounts while delegating D accounts to social media or mass marketing efforts without direct sales involvement, except for walk-in customers. Such strategic approaches may prompt a comprehensive rethink of your dealership's sales organization and assignment processes. Questions arise, such as which A accounts should be visited quarterly by the sales team – a team comprising the account salesperson, service manager, sales manager, and, for high-priority accounts, the dealer principal. This level of strategic planning may not apply to C accounts. Have these organizational considerations been discussed with your sales manager?

You probably have unique groups of customers. Each sector demands unique sales approaches, often necessitating different salespeople or teams. Yet, within each market phase, an opportunity exists to foster closer relationships and enhance profits by showcasing the benefits of transitioning to the next phase of the evolving market. Take consumers, for example; while most fall into Phase II, could we demonstrate the advantages of our Phase III services to some of them? Even those solely concerned with price could be presented with a package encompassing purchase price, annual service, and resale value as a monthly fixed rate (lease).

Not every consumer may opt for this, but capturing some for monthly revenue, future-dated trade-ins, and future equipment sales can prove invaluable. Each market phase has the potential to transition seamlessly to the next, presenting a continuum of opportunities.

Your approach of balancing growth aspirations with a keen understanding of practical constraints positions your sales for long-term success. If there are specific aspects you'd like to delve deeper into or if you have any specific questions, feel free to share. Your strategic understanding is evident in navigating the complexities of market dynamics and customer engagement.

Account Acquisition vs. Account Penetration

Opting for a different strategy, the second choice involves account penetration. In this approach, the aim is to secure a substantial portion, if not all, of the end-user business within a smaller customer segment. This stands in contrast to the broader reach of selling to numerous customers. The penetration strategy necessitates a heightened focus on customers and delivering the value package consistently emphasized.

The accompanying graphs visually represent the two strategies: acquisition and penetration. The account acquisition strategy aims to reach as many accounts as feasible, whereas account penetration centers on consolidating the entirety of a customer's business rather than expanding to a larger pool of end users..

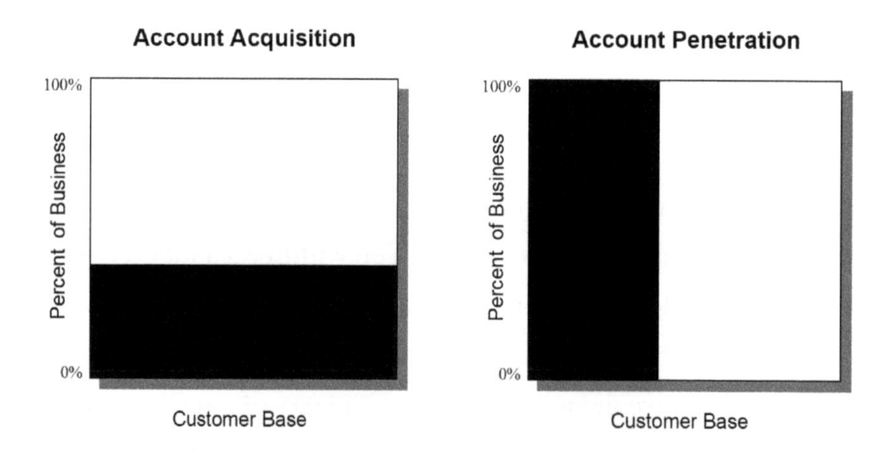

ACQUIRING ACCOUNTS IS ABOUT CREATING SOLUTIONS AND NOT ABOUT SELLING.

In reality, dealerships end up with some mix of accounts at varying levels of penetration resulting in a portfolio resembling the following graph:

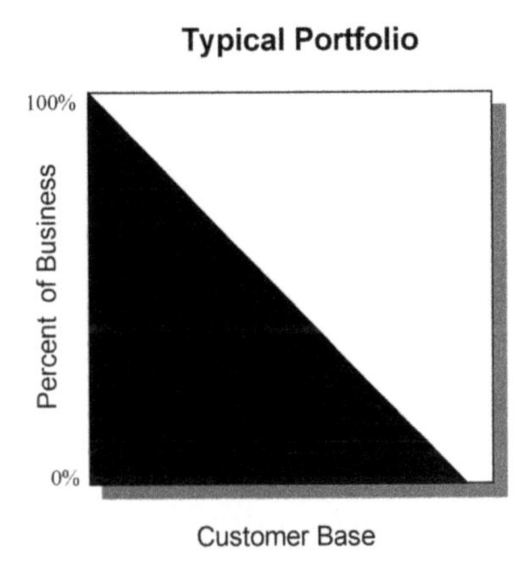

Distributor principals are faced with the decision of selecting a strategy. Wise Wolf Consultants advocate for the advantages of a penetration approach. While not discouraging the sale to smaller or less likely 100% capture accounts, we assert that it shouldn't be the primary focus. Acquiring the entirety of a customer's business yields maximum benefits in parts, service, and rental business. It also grants significant control over unit replacements, establishing a formidable barrier against competitors. When a customer is entirely committed to a specific dealership, the switching costs become a deterrent, making it improbable for the customer to shift to a competitor unless mishandled by the dealer/distributor.

Quality Factors:

Continuous reinforcement of the quality message within the customer base is imperative for the distribution organization. Building competency and enhancing quality in other areas, such as parts, service, and rental, is essential. As customers increasingly look to the dealer/distributor as their exclusive provider, readiness to offer superior products and services becomes paramount to maintaining these accounts.

The Quality Factors for most dealerships are generated from the aftermarket. Since an equipment sale is more transactional, the aftermarket is an ongoing frequency. The parts availability, first-time completion of service repair, the scheduled maintenance execution, and rental availability all contribute to the perception of quality to a customer.

Penetration Strategy Execution:

After completing the initial steps of identifying and acquiring an account and deciding to pursue an account penetration strategy, the focus shifts to delivering superior service to the account. By consistently delivering quality and value, penetration with the account is built, fostering the development of an alliance. Over time, both parties may express the desire to formalize the relationship. This leads to your next step – Contractual Relationships.

Contract Relationship

Every dealer/distributor boasts a specific clientele who have not only chosen them but have also formalized the relationship through service contracts. End users wouldn't commit to such agreements unless they had confidence in the dealer/distributor's ability to service their equipment and were satisfied with past performance.

Account Alliance

These service contracts serve as a crucial revenue stream, providing essential support for the business's ongoing operations. Consistently delivering superior service reinforces customer satisfaction and enables the acquisition of more contractual business. This, in turn, results in a continuous revenue stream—a reliable influx of revenue every month. A dependable monthly revenue is a significant asset for any business, contributing to stability and allowing for strategic planning.

Contracts (or paper agreements) are only as strong as the two parties that make them. But on your part, you can strengthen that commitment through your own communication and involvement with the customer. Beyond the "agreement/contract," how often do you actually sit down with your customer to discuss the results of your work for them? Discuss with them the impact of your proactive work, the reasons for your repair work, and your recommendations of what will help them manage their expenses.

Financial Model

Even when not written, the contracts develop the revenue stream. But as an equipment dealership, you have multiple revenue streams.

There are revenues from equipment sales, rentals, parts sales, and service work, to name the most obvious.

Revenue Stream

You need a structure to manage these revenue streams for profit.

The Financial Model for sales is shown here. It should be noted that expenses and operating profit are shown as a percentage of gross profit, unlike the other areas, where they are shown in terms of revenue. There are several reasons for this approach.

	Sales	Parts	Service	Rental	G&A**
Sales		100%	100%	100%	
Gross Profit	100%	35%	65%	45%	
Expenses*					
Personnel	50%	10%	20%	10%	5%
Operating	25%	3%	10%	7%	3%
Occupancy	10%	2%	5%	3%	2%
Total Expenses	85%	15%	35%	20%	10%
Operating Profit	15%	20%	30%	25%	-10%

Personnel Expenses

First, personnel expenses in the sales department are largely a function of commissions paid to sales representatives as a percentage of gross profit earned on a sale. Also, by pegging department spending to the gross profit generated, we discourage the salespeople and the sales manager from taking low-margin deals. The tendency in any business is to spend what is allocated.

If we set the expense benchmarks as a percent of revenue, the natural inclination is to increase revenue. However, in the sales department, this often equates to reducing the profit margin on the units sold to win a sale we may have otherwise passed on.

You will need to determine the expected gross profit in the sales area for your industry and your market area. For example, we expect an average of 12% gross margin in a material handling dealer/distributor and 14% gross margin in a construction dealership.

The sales department's sales cost should include the acquisition, delivery, and preparation costs for the complete units. All other costs should go into one of the expense categories.

The Financial Model allocates 50% of gross profit to personnel expenses. These expenses include salaries, wages, commissions, bonuses, benefits, insurance, payroll taxes, etc. The dealer/distributor can decide how this 50% is allocated among salespeople, sales administration, sales manager, and benefits. We provide some guidelines that, in our experience, provide an equitable and effective mix.

Sales Manager	7%
Sales Salary & Commissions	30%
Sales Administration	5%
Benefits	8%
Total Personnel	50%

Again, these percentages are a percentage of the gross profit earned in the sales department. It is widely acknowledged that benefits account for about 20% of all personnel costs. Therefore, 50% divided by 1.2 gives us 42% of the GP$ for salary, wages, and commissions, leaving 8% for benefits. The question now is how to allocate the 50%. Each of the percentages listed above is a guideline. Each dealer/distributor principal/sales manager must decide how to compensate sales employees.

Salespeople are almost universally paid through salary and commission. If we expect $240,000 in gross profit from a salesperson, then we will pay $72,000 in commissions if we want to hold the 30% figure for salespeople. Maybe you want to pay a lower commission and give the salesperson a chance to earn an incentive at the end of the year. Each dealer/distributor must make this decision.

In this example, the sales manager is paid 7% of gross profit. This puts the burden and the responsibility of sales department performance on the sales manager. If he wants to know how to make more money, the answer is simple: "Make gross profit dollars go up."

If GP goes down, he will make less money. Whether this means that the sales manager sends all the salespeople out to the large accounts with more volume but skinny margins or focuses on the "C Accounts" with higher margins but less volume, this is not the real issue.

The strategy is sound as long as everyone in the sales department is focused on making gross profit dollars go up. When we look at sales administration, we allocate 5% of gross profit to cover these salaries. The actual figure depends on how much we pay the admin people and how much support our salespeople require. Suppose we can function with an admin staff that only costs 4% of GP, that would be excellent. A general rule is one administrative person for every three outside salespeople.

Each dealer/distributor should review their staffing requirements as inside salespeople's structure and job scope seem to vary widely. We may want to add a line to the above table specifically for inside salespeople. Some businesses have the inside people handling only parts. There is not enough consensus or consistency at this point to establish a firm rule in this area.

We want to get back to the point that the ultimate decision on compensation belongs to the dealer/distributor principal. The Financial Model does not intend to provide benchmarks at such a micro level. Issues such as compensation are a function of the businesses' strategies and philosophy. We intend to assert that, whatever compensation strategy is implemented, the total expense should not exceed 50% of the sales department's gross profit.

Operating Expense

Operating expenses are expected to be 25% or less of sales gross profit. Operating expenses should include those expenses that do not fit into personnel or occupancy expenses (as described below). These items tend to be very clear-cut, especially once personnel and occupancy expenses have been defined.

Occupancy Expense

Occupancy should not exceed 10% of the sales department's gross profit. This category includes rent, lease, utilities (excluding telephone, which should be included in operating expenses), property taxes, improvements, etc. Anything to do with the facility or its upkeep should be considered occupancy expense.

From a performance point of view, we need to be careful about allocating occupancy expenses since this can rarely be done based on actual usage.

It would be unusual to find a dealer/distributor with a separate electric meter for the service shop, parts warehouse, office areas, etc.

Since rent or lease payments tend to be the most significant expense, it might make sense to do this allocation based on the actual percentage (by square footage) used by each department. Then, other occupancy costs, such as insurance and taxes, would follow the same allocation scheme. Utility usage will not work out perfectly using this approach, but it should be close enough to be fair to all departments. We do not want to punish managers for a factor out of their control.

Target Equity

Investment

For a well-managed business that meets financial benchmarks, this consistent cash flow generated from service contracts, equipment sales, rental business, etc., becomes a source of funds for sustainable growth. The ability to count on regular revenue month after month is a critical element in the professional and financial success of the business.

Once you have your revenue stream organized and structured for profits, you then turn to managing the assets or investment to handle this investment correctly. As the investor/owner, you want to utilize the investment to obtain the maximum return. That might mean you are over-invested in the current business. Then, you would look to reduce your inventory, accounts receivable, and other assets to an appropriate level. Generally, we recommend achieving about three turns on your assets.

If you have excess investment, you might expand your territory, working on gaining more market share. You might consider taking on more product lines that complement your existing business or are complimentary to your existing customer base. Suppose you don't see an opportunity to expand your current business or product lines. In that case, this might be a time to remove cash/investment from your business and put it in your personal assets.

Conclusion

Envisioned as a spiral staircase, the Fundamental Business Strategy involves traversing an iterative loop, ascending to higher levels with each cycle. The overarching objective of each iteration is to enhance business volume through account acquisition and penetration while optimizing profitability. This conceptual model is then translated to the operational realm, where each department is systematically discussed, encompassing profit contributions, operational considerations, benchmarks, staffing, and critical departmental variables.

This transition represents a significant opportunity for dealers/distributors. Historically centered on products and sales, with services provided out of necessity, the organization can capitalize on the profitability of service, parts, and rental operations when managed effectively. When combined with robust profit margins on equipment, adeptly managed service and parts departments can propel most dealers/distributors toward a noteworthy 8-10% operating income.

To seize this opportunity, the initial step is to ensure adequate coverage of accounts within the territory. The requisite marketing and sales capabilities can be developed by diligently following the account management process, progressing towards account assignment, expanding the sales force, evolving into a proactive sales organization, and shifting from a product-centric approach to a customer solutions focus.

Remember that once we begin to generate the revenue stream, we must manage that revenue stream against an expected level of financial performance. This provides cash flow to reinvest in the business and continue the account acquisition and penetration process.

4. Characteristics of Successful Sales Organizations

Vision Statement and Successful Dealer/Distributor:

Once the Vision Statement is established, the question arises: What constitutes a successful dealer/distributor when it's 'right'? Prioritizing 'right' over perfect, the Value Delivery Vision equips you with tools to manage and enhance profitability, enabling informed decision-making.

Characteristics of Successful Companies:

Common challenges in various client scenarios often center around broad business aspects such as culture, mission, and long-term plans. When effectively defined and implemented, these factors contribute to companies' success. These are known as the "Characteristics of Successful Companies," ultimately gauged by the return on investment.

Fundamentals of Management:

Foundational management principles are indispensable. Managing entails changing behavior, and robust, effective leadership is pivotal for success. The analogy of a manager as a coach underscores the importance of having a clear game plan, aligning the team, and addressing performance gaps.

Developing the Game Plan:

Precisely identifying and communicating the game plan is the initial challenge for managers aiming for behavioral change. Developing awareness and understanding of the plan becomes crucial. While a design is provided, it's essential to customize it to the unique circumstances of each business.

Knowledge and Skill Building:

After communicating the plan, attention shifts to building internal competencies. Identifying gaps in knowledge and skills becomes paramount.

Training, development, and educational programs are implemented to bridge these gaps, ensuring personnel are equipped to execute the plan.

Reinforcement Methods:

The next step involves reinforcing expected performance. Positive reinforcement, negative reinforcement, and punishment are discussed. Positive reinforcement is highlighted as more effective, with caution against saturating employees with excessive praise.

Three Steps for Behavioral Change:

The overall process for managers aiming at behavioral change involves three steps: developing a business plan and raising awareness, ensuring employees have necessary skills and knowledge, and establishing a system for reinforcing desirable behavior to maintain employee motivation.

Focus Issues for Successful Organizations:

A successful organization requires a sense of focus, both internally and within the manufacturer-dealer alliance. The term 'partnership' is avoided, emphasizing that each dealer/distributor is its own business. The alliance's success is contingent on managing individual dealerships effectively and maintaining alignment in focus to prevent conflicts.

Culture Issues

Organizational culture encompasses a collection of values that shape an organization's operational framework and qualitative attributes. Every organization inherently carries a culture, and if allowed to develop organically, it can either embrace mediocrity or cultivate an environment that encourages excellence. It becomes the responsibility of management to proactively influence the evolution of organizational culture, guiding it towards a structure that harmonizes with and bolsters the attainment of the organization's goals. In a flourishing organization, the culture is distinguished by a dedication to intensity and a hunger for the work, playing a significant role in its overall success.

Culture Issues	
■ Mission	■ Concern for People
■ Intensity	■ Customer Orientation
■ Quality of Leadership	■ Pride
■ Continuous Improvement	

Mission

Diverse opinions exist regarding the importance of a mission statement. Often, these statements may sound generic and end up as mere adornments on the wall, eventually forgotten in storage. Regardless of the terminology, every organization should possess a statement that encapsulates its mission and objectives. All employees must have the opportunity to contribute to developing this statement, and management should meticulously review it to ensure everyone comprehends its content and intent. Mission statements transcend mere phrases when employees grasp and believe in their content.

> In conjunction with the mission statement, there's the business scorecard. Can every employee walk into a shared space or a manager's office and assess the team's performance for the month, quarter, or year-to-date? The mission is crucial, as is the ability to continually measure oneself. The organization must have a clear direction, and employees must gauge their progress toward reaching the destination.

Intensity

Another pivotal aspect within an organization is cultivating intensity—a passionate drive to succeed. The objective is not to create tension but to nurture an environment where individuals are motivated to excel. When a customer makes a call, someone on the other end should be eager to address their needs. Intensity should be a shared attribute across the entire organization, transcending positions and functions. Every employee, regardless of their role, should embody intensity.

Every individual within the building plays a vital role for the organization to function seamlessly, and each employee should recognize the significance of their contribution.

If someone's role is not integral to the operation, questions arise about their purpose within the organization.

Leadership

Evaluating the quality of leadership can be a complex task, yet its impact is unmistakable when observed. In a previous discussion, we delved into the basics of management. Now, let's explore how effective leadership integrates with these principles.

Exceptional leaders inspire a shared vision. They not only craft a vision but also effectively communicate it to everyone. A leader's delivery of this vision should be inspirational, marked by sincerity, integrity, and intensity that conveys a sense of purpose. This doesn't require flamboyance but demands a genuine and compelling articulation of what the organization stands for. How well is management fostering a shared vision within the organization?

Successful leaders not only inspire a shared vision but consistently challenge the process. Drawing a parallel to a team's dynamics with the manager as a coach, positive reinforcement is crucial after a game. However, a good leader doesn't stop there; they challenge the team to identify areas for improvement and strive for continuous progress.

Empowering people to act is a hallmark of effective leadership. Discerning which decisions need top-level attention and which can be delegated to frontline employees is a skill that effective leaders possess. As employees demonstrate their capability, a good leader willingly delegates more responsibilities down the organizational hierarchy.

Modeling the way is a straightforward principle: leaders exemplify the behavior they wish to see in others. Employees tend to emulate the actions and reactions of management. Therefore, the conduct of leaders significantly shapes the organizational culture.

Celebrating victories is vital for morale and organizational success. Acknowledging achievements, explaining areas of excellence, and expressing gratitude to the team contribute to a positive work environment. Equally important is refraining from celebrations during challenging periods, fostering a mindset of improvement and a commitment to achieving goals.

In summary, effective leaders inspire a shared vision, challenge the process, empower others, model the way, and celebrate victories. Evaluating the presence of these characteristics in your organization is critical. Encouraging managers to lead effectively is pivotal; employees are more likely to follow suit when leadership is strong. It's incumbent upon managers to exhibit the desired characteristics, setting the tone for the entire organization.

Continuous Improvement

Encouraging continuous improvement in processes requires a concerted effort to engage employees and foster an environment where feedback is valued. Several strategies can be employed to enhance employee involvement and make managers comfortable with receiving feedback:

Quality Teams: Establish quality teams that bring together your salespeople to collaborate on identifying and implementing improvements and looking deeper into your customer relationships. These teams can serve as a forum for sharing insights and ideas, approaches that have worked in building relationships, and times they have missed the mark and lost a customer.

Departmental Meetings: Regular departmental meetings provide a platform for salespeople to discuss challenges, propose solutions, and contribute their perspectives. Managers should actively encourage open dialogue and consider employee suggestions seriously. In dealerships I have worked in, there was either a Monday morning meeting each week or a Tuesday if that works better for you.

Feedback Mechanisms: Implement formal feedback mechanisms that allow salespeople to submit suggestions, concerns, or ideas anonymously if preferred. This can help salespeople feel more comfortable sharing their thoughts without fear of reprisal. As a sales manager, you must use every tool you have to succeed.

Recognition and Rewards: Recognize and reward your sales team for contributing to process improvement. This can include acknowledging their efforts in team meetings, providing incentives, or instituting a salesperson of the month program. Of course, you are using a commission plan that should be recognized, but salespeople enjoy being recognized in front of their peers.

Training Programs: Offer training programs that empower employees with the skills necessary for process improvement. This can include problem-solving techniques, critical thinking, and methodologies such as Six Sigma or Lean.

Leadership Example: Leaders should exemplify a culture of continuous improvement by actively seeking feedback. When salespeople see that managers are open to suggestions and committed to improvement, they are more likely to participate. In the market share chapter, consider the discussion of traveling with your salespeople on calls.

Clear Communication: Managers should communicate clearly about the importance of continuous improvement and how employee involvement contributes to the organization's overall success. Transparency builds trust and encourages collaboration.

Pilot Projects: Initiate small-scale pilot projects where teams can test and implement improvements in a controlled environment. This allows for experimentation without disrupting the entire operation. Consider establishing a team to work on one large account. It might be a new experience for the salespeople, but if it's only one account, they will not feel like you're trying to change their entire experience in selling.

Celebrate Success: When improvements lead to positive outcomes, celebrate the success as a team. This reinforces the value of employee contributions and encourages a culture of continuous improvement.

By implementing these strategies, organizations can create an environment where employees feel empowered to contribute to process improvement actively, and managers embrace feedback as a valuable resource for organizational growth.

Concern for People

Managers need to genuinely care about their team members and understand the fundamental elements contributing to employee satisfaction at work. Recognizing the key factors that drive employee contentment is essential. Contrary to common assumptions, a survey by the USA Surgeon General[3] revealed that the most significant factor for employee satisfaction is

---

[3] October 2022 – "Surgeon General's Framework for Workplace Mental Health and Well-Being" 95% said it is very (66%) or somewhat (29%) important to them to feel respected at work.

recognition, while salary and benefits ranked lower on the list. This notable difference from managers' perceptions underscores the significance of comprehending employee priorities.

Demonstrating concern for people involves several essential practices. Clearly articulate and communicate expectations. Employees need to comprehend the purpose behind their tasks and the expected performance standards. Clarity fosters a sense of purpose and direction.

Customer Orientation

A successful organization genuinely prioritizes customer satisfaction, positioning it as a primary goal. While many dealerships assert such commitment, the key lies in maintaining an unwavering focus on customer needs. A practical approach involves routinely assessing customer rankings through tools like descending sales reports. These reports organize customers from highest to lowest based on sales volume, providing a comprehensive view of customer dynamics.

The descending sales report serves as a crucial tool for identifying key customers and detecting changes in their rankings. For instance, a significant drop from 27th to 87th for a customer warrants attention and proactive measures. When such shifts occur, it becomes crucial for management, at an appropriate level, to engage with the customer. This engagement could involve a visit or communication to understand the factors contributing to the decline in ranking.

Proactive customer engagement reflects a commitment to addressing their concerns and maintaining a robust customer-centric approach. These detailed reports are critical in highlighting shifts in customer dynamics and provide valuable insights. Regular assessments empower organizations to adapt, strengthen ties with key customers, and promptly address customer satisfaction issues.

In essence, the utilization of descending sales reports goes beyond merely asserting customer orientation. It becomes a strategic tool for staying attuned to customer satisfaction, identifying trends, and ensuring timely actions to preserve and enhance customer relationships.

95% said it is very (61%) or somewhat (34%) important to them to work for an organization that respects the boundaries between work and nonwork time.

Pride

A final and crucial element involves taking pride in our work, building, business, and more. What message does it convey when we approach the parking lot and cast our eyes on the building? What does it communicate about the individuals working there? As we step through the door, whether into the administrative area, service zone, or warehouse, what impressions are formed about the workforce? If there's a palpable sense of pride in the environment, signaling that it is well-maintained, it serves as positive reinforcement. Conversely, adjustments may be necessary if sentiments suggest neglect or convey a perception of management frugality. Perhaps a collective effort on a Saturday morning involves painting the administrative area, sprucing up the shop, or enhancing the front of the building.

The facility's appearance is merely one example of how pride becomes evident. It also manifests in employees' demeanor, handling telephone calls, and even in the aesthetics of their internal or external correspondence. Pride might be challenging to quantify, but the presence or absence of organizational pride is something we can discern.

Summary

The emphasis on focus issues naturally leads to outlining objectives, goals, and measurements. An organization with a strong focus tends to be highly quantitative, while qualitative characteristics within the organization primarily shape culture. A meticulously planned and well-engineered organization with a weak culture—lacking passion and intensity—may generate excellent plans but struggle with implementation. Conversely, an organization with a robust culture—marked by abundant passion and intensity—yet lacking clear direction can become a source of internal frustration. Meanwhile, an organization devoid of passion and intensity and a lack of direction is destined for failure.

Returning to the fundamental importance of culture, especially in intensity and passion, we recognize that culture is challenging, if not impossible, to measure precisely due to its qualitative nature. However, a thriving organization adeptly balances qualitative and quantitative attributes, thus constructing a comprehensive and well-rounded business.

5. Sales Department Critical Variables

Establishing the standard, like a golfer aiming to compete professionally must consistently shoot par, is fundamental in any business. Winning championships requires surpassing par by a significant margin in most cases. The same principle applies to external factors like mushy fairways, adverse wind, rain, or personal conditions, which don't alter the par designation on a golf course. Whether the business environment is challenging or favorable, the financial benchmarks for a professionally managed dealer/distributor remain consistent, as outlined in the Financial Model.

From a financial perspective, the Financial Model represents the benchmark for a well-operated dealer/distributor. It's not a one-time target or an ideal applicable to every business. Instead, it exemplifies what the financial landscape should look like when everything is optimized. While individual companies may adjust specific figures, the emphasis is on maintaining or exceeding this level of profitability or dealership best practices. The overarching goal is to avoid regression.

Segmentation for Clarity:

To thoroughly understand each aspect of performance, the Financial Model breaks down the business into distinct departments. While a consolidated income statement can point out general issues like low gross profit or high expenses, the real insights and opportunities for improvement become apparent when the business is analyzed in separate components. This is similar to how a technician pinpoints problems in a malfunctioning machine by examining each part individually.

Segmenting the business in this way allows for a more detailed and focused analysis of each department, making it easier to identify specific areas for adjustments and enhancements. Just as precise diagnosis is crucial for fixing a machine, understanding each business component is essential for effective management and long-term success.

To achieve this, each department is evaluated based on certain key variables:

Department Critical Variables	
■ Market Share ■ Financial Control	■ Asset Utilization ■ Productivity ■ Satisfaction Rating

As we noted earlier, market share and quality are two key drivers of return on assets. Therefore, we focus on driving market share in all product areas: sales, service, parts, and rental. The remaining items are also essential in every area of the business. Each department also has specific variables related to its function. This book will discuss only critical variables for the sales department.

	Sales	Parts	Service	Rental	G&A**
Sales		100%	100%	100%	
Gross Profit	100%	35%	65%	45%	
Expenses*					
Personnel	50%	10%	20%	10%	5%
Operating	25%	3%	10%	7%	3%
Occupancy	10%	2%	5%	3%	2%
Total Expenses	85%	15%	35%	20%	10%
Operating Profit	15%	20%	30%	25%	-10%

Gross Profit

It's key to note that in this context, expenses and operating profit are measured as a percentage of gross profit, rather than the usual practice of basing them on revenue. This method is chosen for several reasons.

Firstly, in the sales department, personnel costs, which largely consist of commissions, are directly linked to the gross profit made on sales. This connection to gross profit discourages sales staff and managers from chasing deals with slim profit margins, reflecting the common practice of spending within allocated limits.

Using revenue as a basis for setting expense benchmarks might lead to a focus on boosting revenue. However, this can often result in diminished profit margins in the sales department, as deals are made on less profitable terms just to increase revenue.

Understanding the expected gross profit in sales is essential and varies by industry and market conditions. For example, a material handling dealer/distributor might expect an average gross margin of 12%, a construction dealership might target around 14%, and other industries could see margins of 20-25%. The sales department's cost of sales should include the acquisition, delivery, and preparation expenses for complete units, with all other costs classified as expenses. Since gross profit calculations are usually more straightforward, discussions can then focus on other critical factors in the sales department: effective expense management, sales productivity, and asset utilization.

Position	Allocated %
Sales Manager	7%
Sales Salary & Commissions	30%
Sales Administration	5%
Benefits	8%
Total Personnel	**50%**

These percentages are calculated from the sales department's gross profit. Benefits are generally about 20% of total personnel costs, so dividing 50% by 1.2 gives us 42% of gross profit for salaries, wages, and commissions, with 8% left for benefits. Deciding how to split this 50% is up to each dealer/distributor principal, who must determine their sales staff's compensation structure.

Salespeople are often paid through a mix of salary and commission. For instance, if a salesperson is expected to generate $240,000 in gross profit, using the 30% guideline would result in $72,000 in compensation. The option to offer a lower commission with potential year-end bonuses is at the discretion of each dealer/distributor.

In our example, the sales manager receives 7% of the gross profit, placing responsibility for sales department performance squarely on their shoulders. The goal is to boost earnings by increasing gross profit dollars. The focus could be on large accounts with high volumes and lower margins or smaller "C Accounts" with higher margins. The key is to enhance gross profit dollars, regardless of the approach.

For sales administration, 5% of the gross profit is set aside for salaries, though this can vary based on administrative staff salaries and the level of support needed for salespeople. A rough guideline is one administrative person for every three outside salespeople.

Each dealer/distributor should evaluate their staffing needs, especially since the role of inside salespeople can differ significantly. Depending on their specific duties, like managing only parts, an additional line for inside sales might be necessary.

Ultimately, compensation decisions rest with the dealer/distributor principal. The Financial Model doesn't prescribe detailed benchmarks but offers guidance. Compensation strategies depend on each business's unique strategies and philosophy, with the overall rule being that total expenses shouldn't exceed 50% of the sales department's gross profit.

Operational Expense:

Anticipated to be 25% or less of sales gross profit, operating expense covers items that don't fall under personnel or occupancy expense, as detailed below. These operational costs become distinctly apparent once personnel and occupancy expenses are defined.

Occupancy Expense:

Occupancy expenses, limited to 10% of the sales department's gross profit, cover various facility-related costs such as rent, lease, utilities (excluding telephone), property taxes, and improvements.

Allocating these expenses demands thoughtful consideration, especially since actual usage measurement is challenging due to shared spaces like service shops, parts warehouses, and offices.

Typically, rent or lease payments are the largest part of these costs. A logical method for allocation might be based on the square footage each department occupies. This method could also apply to other occupancy expenses like insurance and taxes. While utility costs might not align perfectly with square footage, this approach usually provides a fair distribution across departments. The goal is to ensure that managers aren't unfairly burdened by costs they can't control.In the last 35 years I've seen many allocation methodologies utilized, including counting the number of cars in the parking lot by department. In practice, we find that Occupancy Expense seldom goes beyond the limits set in the Financial Model. Thus, distributing these costs among departments should not overly strain departmental managers.

Employee Productivity:

Anticipating a competent and fully trained salesperson, we expect they would generate a minimum of $240,000 per year in gross profit within an equipment dealership. This benchmark applies to various sectors: material handling at $240,000, and agricultural equipment or power generation at $240,000, with potential variations in other industries. It's important to note that these benchmarks are derived solely from selling new and used machines. However, considering the presence of new or underperforming salespeople, the actual ratio may vary. Moreover, accepting deals with diverse gross margins further contributes to this variation. While most companies wouldn't forego a $500,000 job even at a 4% or 5% gross profit, some deals may yield a more favorable 10-15% gross profit.

Asset Utilization:

We advocate that the sales department manage the dealer/distributor's unit inventory. This strategic approach enables management to assess departmental performance in terms of profit and loss and asset utilization. In evaluating a dealer/distributor's sales department, three crucial asset measurements come into play.

	Construction	Material Handling	Agricultural Equipment	Air Compressors	Golf Cars
New Inventory Turns	9 Turns	12 Turns	4 Turns	6 Turns	4 Turns
Used Inventory Turns	4 Turns	6 Turns	3 Turns	3 Turns	6 Turns
Inventory Aging	0%	0%	0%	0%	0%

Inventory Turnover:

The frequency with which we revolve our machine inventory serves as a measure of the precision and efficiency of the company's inventory management. We expect the company to achieve a turnover of its stock inventory, but based on the industry, industry seasonality and manufacturer supply scheduling this can be drastically different.

Addressing Non-Moving Inventory:

Non-moving inventory, such as used items or trade-acquired machines, often leads to unnecessary expenses. These units not only incur interest costs but also take up valuable storage space. This type of inventory also locks up capital that could be better used in other business areas. It's crucial to sell these items within twelve months to avoid obsolescence due to technological advances, which can make them hard to sell. When these items do sell, they typically require significant markdowns, which can eat into profit margins.

Assigning Responsibility to the Sales Manager:

You're absolutely right in pointing out that traditionally, issues like customer satisfaction and loyalty tend to be handled by higher management levels, often tucked away under general expenses in the budget. However, this approach can sometimes mask the real impact these factors have on the overall health and success of the organization.

Shifting the responsibility to sales managers can indeed be a game-changer. Think of it like giving the keys of a powerful car to someone who's only been riding a bicycle.

Suddenly, they have the power to drive significant improvements, but they need to understand how to use that power effectively.

Educating sales managers about the broader impact of their role is crucial. It's not just about hitting sales targets anymore. It's about understanding how their actions affect the organization's overall profit and loss. This perspective can lead to a more holistic approach to sales, where every decision is weighed not just for its immediate sales impact, but for its long-term effects on the company's health.

Moreover, integrating profit and loss considerations with inventory control and management within the sales department acknowledges the interconnected nature of these facets. It's like recognizing that every part of a watch works together to tell time. Sales, inventory, and financial health are deeply interlinked, and understanding these connections can lead to more informed, strategic decision-making.

By empowering sales managers in this way, organizations can foster a more proactive and responsible approach to sales and customer relationships, leading to healthier profits and a more robust company culture. This is about breaking down silos within the organization and encouraging a more integrated, team-oriented approach to business success.

Customer Satisfaction

Maintaining and improving customer satisfaction is what creates customer loyalty. Many people have stated and quoted costs to keep customers and replace ones that are lost.

It sounds like the airline industry has been having a rough time, doesn't it? It's like everything that could go wrong, did go wrong for them. Employees who aren't happy with their jobs, skyrocketing fuel costs, some companies even facing bankruptcy, and then to top it off, a mountain of issues with luggage. It's no wonder their customer satisfaction took a nosedive!

Talking about customer satisfaction isn't just a casual chat over coffee, it's super important. Think about it like this: It's one of those secret ingredients that the most successful businesses, like top-notch dealers and distributors, always have in their recipe for success.

J.D. POWER 2023 NORTH AMERICAN AIRLINE SATISFACTION

OVERALL PASSENGER SATISFACTION BASED ON A 1,000 POINT SCALE

First/Business	
JetBlue	893
Delta	865
United	848
Average	*846*
Alaska	833
Air Canada	830
American	826

Premium Economy	
Delta	848
JetBlue	840
Alaska	823
American	821
Average	*820*
Air Canada	797
United	784

Economy/Basic Economy	
Southwest	827
Delta	801
JetBlue	800
Average	*782*
Alaska	781
WestJet	777
Allegiant	775
United	770
Air Canada	765
American	764
Spirit	727
Frontier	705

Source: J.D. Power

They know that making customers happy is just as crucial as making a profit, having productive employees, or grabbing a big chunk of the market.

> Annual declines in passenger satisfaction were most pronounced in the economy/basic economy segments, according to the report. Satisfaction with cost and fees for this segment dropped 19 points from a year ago, and of the 11 carriers ranked, WestJet was the only airline to show an improvement, moving from 751 to 777, or to fifth place from last place in 2022.
>
> Taken from Business Traveler News by North Travel Group May 10, 2023

But here's the catch – you can't just focus on making your customers smile while letting everything else slide. It's like trying to ride a bike with only one wheel. Sure, you might manage for a little bit, but eventually, you're going to crash.

You need to balance customer happiness with making money, having a great team, and holding onto a good market share.

And guess what USA Today pointed out about the airlines? The number one issue they highlighted was unhappy employees. It's a huge red flag. It's like asking yourself, "Do my employees actually enjoy working here? Do they feel proud to be part of the team?" When things go sideways with customers – maybe they're grumbling about prices, delivery times, or product quality – do your employees go to bat for the company? Or do they just nod along with the customer's complaints?

This is crucial because your employees are your front line. They're the ones interacting with your customers every day. If they're not happy, or if they don't believe in the value of what they're selling, it's going to be really hard to keep your customers happy and your business thriving.

Employee satisfaction will drive customer satisfaction like no other factor in your company.

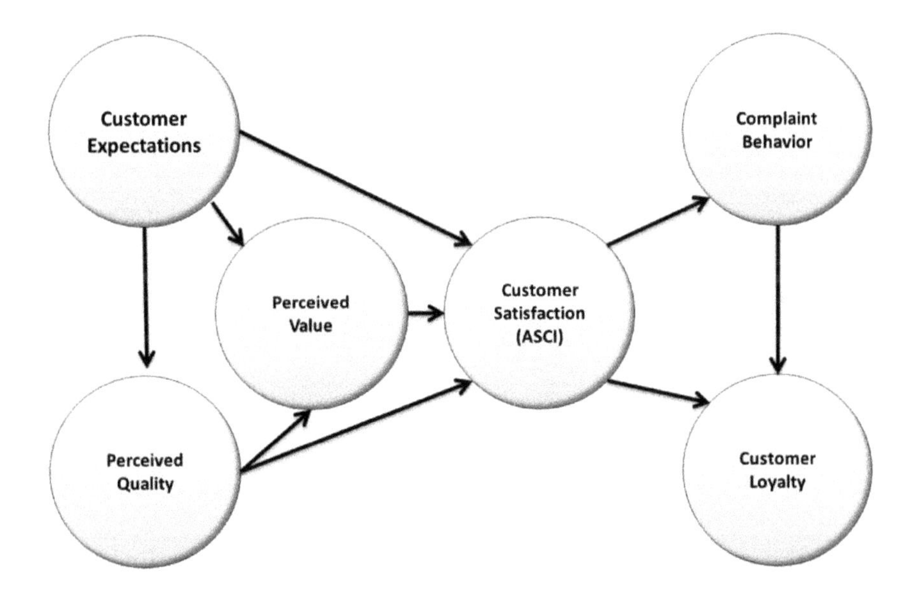

The University of Michigan American Customer Satisfaction Index[4] has designed a model of Customer Satisfaction. What is interesting about this diagram is that it also works the same when you replace the word "customer" with "employee." So, are you working on creating employee satisfaction?

Employee satisfaction should be measured, like customer satisfaction, but it can also be developed and controlled. Have you defined the "job and responsibilities" of the employee? You need to make these clear, measurable, and attainable. Then you need to communicate progress and accomplishment. Next, you need to provide recognition or positive feedback on the behavior and success.

[4] National Quality Research Center. "The American Customer Satisfaction Index: The Voice of the Nation's Consumer." 2006. Stephen M. Ross Business School, University of Michigan, Ann Arbor, MI. Type of Work: Web Site. Accessed from http://www.theacsi.org/overview.htm.

Absolutely, you've hit the nail on the head with how loyalty and satisfaction work wonders, both for customers and employees. It's like when you've got customers who are not just satisfied, but truly delighted with what you offer, they're not just buying your products – they're buying into your brand. They stop looking around for better deals because they trust you. They see the real value in what you're providing, beyond just the price tag. It's like they've moved from just casual dating to being in a committed relationship with your company.

This kind of loyalty means they'll likely buy a wider range of products from you, not just the ones that are priced competitively. They're less focused on getting the cheapest deal and more on the quality and value you're offering. This isn't just good news; it's great news for your business. It means more stable and possibly higher revenue from these loyal customers.

Now, let's talk about the cost of losing a customer. It's like when you've built a beautiful house of cards and then one card slips – the effort to rebuild can be massive. Losing a customer and then having to find a new one can burn a hole in your pocket, costing thousands, depending on how valuable they were and how tough they are to replace.

That's why for sales managers, it's not just a job, it's a mission to create and keep these delighted customers. It's about nurturing that relationship, understanding their needs, and consistently delivering value that goes above and beyond. It's like being a gardener where your customers are the plants; you need to water them, give them sunlight, and care for them, so they grow strong and stay healthy.

Summary

The pivotal factors influencing sales department profitability encompass managing sales force productivity, financial performance, and asset utilization effectively. The sales manager needs to be accountable for attaining the critical variables within each of these domains. Linking compensation to these performance metrics serves as a mechanism to incentivize the sales manager to take full ownership of all aspects of the department. Beyond the direct profit contribution, a proficiently operated sales department acts as a feeder for the parts, service, and rental departments, generating substantial operating income for the overall business.

Sales Critical Variables

Variables	Benchmark
Operating Profit	15% of GP
Salesperson GP per year productivity (competent)	$240,000 Material Handling
Market share (varies by industry)	25%
New Machine Inventory Turns	8.0 (Financial) 6.0 (Stock)
Non Moving Inventory (12 months)	0%
Customer Satisfaction	90%+

6. Market Share

The Calculation

To enhance profitability, the organization must prioritize maet share. The salesperson's role in this domain is undeniably crucial. Market share can be quantified using the formula below:

$$\text{Awareness X Closure} = \text{Market Share}$$

Explained simply, Awareness is the number of customers and prospects you are in contact with during the time period involved. This could be a single month, quarter, or the full year. In those industries where the manufacturers share delivery information, they collect enough data to identify all units sold/delivered within your AOR (Area of Responsibility). The formula for that is shown as an equation below:

$$\frac{Sales + Lost}{Market} = Awareness$$

To illustrate the formula, your manufacturer sends you a monthly report that says there were 1,000 units sold in your territory. You sold 200 units and lost sales of quotes you presented for another 200 units. Therefore, you were involved in 400 units during that time period, but 1,000 units were sold. So, your Awareness is 40%.

However, awareness is only half of the equation for calculating your market share. The other half is about your efficiency in closing deals. The equation below shows that of the unit deals you were involved in (Sold + Lost in the denominator), you only sold a certain amount. Using our previous example, you sold 200, and you did not close 200 that you quoted. Therefore, your 200 units sold was 50% of the units you were involved in.

$$\frac{Sold}{Sold + Lost} = Closure$$

Stated another way, we can write the entire formula as follows:

$$\frac{\cancel{Sold+Lost}}{Market}\ x\ \frac{Sold}{\cancel{Sold+Lost}} = \frac{Sold}{Market}\ \text{(or Market Share)}$$

Refinements are necessary in our sales tracking processes to calculate market share precisely. Two critical components often lacking in many dealerships are call reports and lost order reports. While monitoring quotes is relatively straightforward, the absence of lost order reports hampers our ability to evaluate close rates on quotes and understand the reasons for quote losses. Similarly, the lack of call reports impedes our grasp of market dynamics, leaving questions unanswered, such as whether an account had a need we didn't quote on or which competitive accounts are currently securing contracts.

Expanding our coverage and implementing the requirement for call reports allows us to enrich the data provided by vendors with local insights, providing a more comprehensive understanding of the local market. Incorporating call reports and lost order reports will undeniably enhance the accuracy and depth of our market share calculations.

We can explore various scenarios by assuming a market share of approximately 30% for this example. Factors such as awareness and close rates that would lead to a 30% market share include the following:

Awareness X Closure = Market Share
90% X 33% = 30%
75% X 40% = 30%
55% X 55% = 30%
40% X 75% = 30%
33% X 90% = 30%

When analyzing these scenarios, which one resonates more closely with your business?

Do your salespeople know of 90% of the deals in your territory but close only one-third of the quotes? Alternatively, are your salespeople closing 90% of the quotes but quoting on just one-third of the jobs? According to our research, a prevalent perception among dealers/distributors suggests that their closing rates typically fall within the 70-80% range, indicating a presence in only 40% of the market.

A close rate of 70-80% is deemed commendable. If this aligns with your situation, the focus should shift towards enhancing market coverage or awareness. This can be accomplished by increasing the number of salespeople and refining market coverage effectiveness through strategies such as account segmentation, account assignment, and the implementation of call frequency schedules. The objective is to optimize market presence and elevate the chances of successful closures.

Understanding the market share calculation is intended to offer insights into where you should direct your efforts. Do you require increased awareness or an improved closing rate? This consideration may vary across territories or among your sales team. We'll discuss this in the chapter on Managing the Sales Force.

What do you do if your manufacturer(s) don't provide this information? While working with one client, we contacted the manufacturer and asked a simple question about how many units (on average) were sold in the entire country. We then compared that number to the total population of the country. That provided how many units for every 1,000 people were sold nationally. Next, we did some research identifying how many people lived in the assigned territory for that dealer. From those simple numbers, we could at least ballpark the expected number of units sold for that smaller population. It certainly is not as scientific as the other method, but it provided some guidelines for that dealer.

Enhancing market share is a continuous and iterative process, continually evolving. Look at this illustration.

The Process

Initiating the process begins in the upper-left corner with Account Identification. Essentially, you inquire whether the company or organization utilizes or requires the type of equipment you offer. It's a fundamental question: are they part of your database of prospects? You're aiming for more than just a name and address; ideally, you seek evidence regarding the number of units they currently have or might require. This could involve a salesperson visiting them, observing visible equipment units, or engaging with the individuals at that location. It could be as simple as a phone call asking someone who answers how many trucks they have.

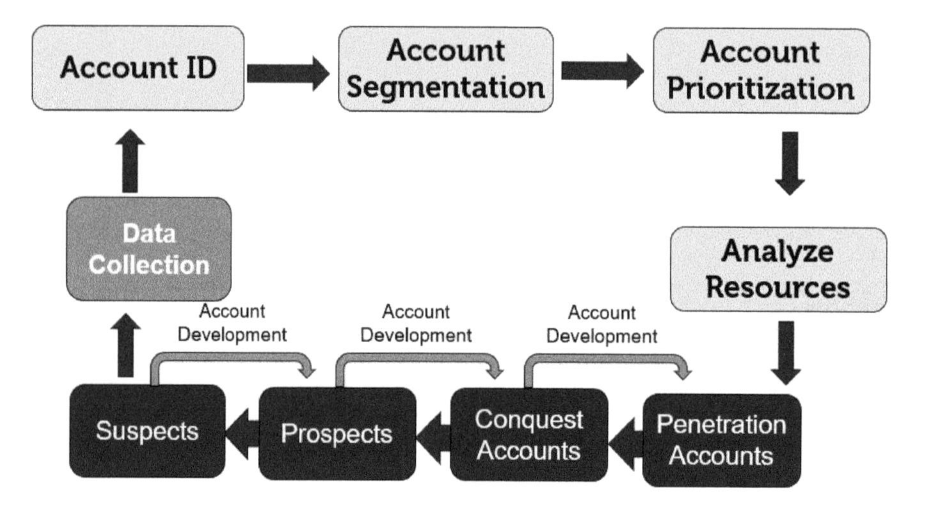

Gathering basic information about prospects is just the starting point. The challenge lies in prioritizing these prospects effectively. Initial calls may not yield detailed insights into their equipment and service expenditures. However, our extensive research on existing dealers' customers over the years reveals a strong correlation between the number of units and the corresponding revenue. This table illustrates this correlation on the next page.

The top 40% of revenue typically stems from approximately 1.5%-3.0% of the accounts. These accounts, characterized as significant users of your product, demand more service and consume a higher volume of replacement parts. While the business concentration might vary across industries, the distribution of the number of units owned or used by accounts generally follows an intuitive pattern. Your unique experiences might introduce slight variations, but overarching similarities should prevail.

Given your resources and available information, a strategic approach involves assessing the account's number of units and estimating the total revenue potential. You can calculate the number of replacement units they might require and project when this need would arise. Additionally, consider potential service revenue, replacement parts consumption, and the likelihood of equipment rentals. Can you then compute the potential gross profit by aggregating the total revenue from these various facets? This exercise aims to determine the value of securing the account as a customer. Calculating this potential with a 5-7 year timeframe would be best. Look at some of your existing accounts over that timeframe also for comparison.

Segment	Revenue Generation	Percent of Accounts	Number of Units Owned or Used
A	Top 40%	3%	25+
B	Next 30%	12%	11-24
C	Next 20%	25%	4-10
D	Final 10%	60%	1-3

Should you identify substantial value, investing time and effort in acquiring this account becomes imperative. Conversely, if the value is not significant, make a note in the account information and redirect your focus to more promising opportunities.

Doing this segmentation will help you get perspective on the value of a prospect. But that is only an initial step in your process of determining how to approach them. If you found a large account, that doesn't mean they will be a good prospect or even a great customer. Your next step should be to Prioritize the account.

We group Priority into three general categories: High, Medium, and Low. Elements to consider in determining Priority could be:

- Location/distance from your dealership
- Revenue Produced in total (or your calculation of potential)
- Their Financial Strength
- Years in Business
- Their Buying Phase
- Other Financial Situations

Factor	Weight	Factor	Weight
Location/Distance		**Credit Rating**	
1-50 Miles	3	Good	3
51-100 Miles	2	Fair	2
101 + Miles	1	Poor	1
Application		**Growth Potential**	
Easy	3	10% +	3
Moderate	2	5-9%	2
Difficult	1	0-4%	1
Buying Phase		**Current Penetration**	
III or IV	3	50% +	3
I	2	25% - 50%	2
II	1	< 25%	1

When evaluating these factors, you may find it beneficial to organize them in a grid for a comparative analysis of multiple prospects or utilize an assessment tool to assign priorities. Take a look at the chart provided for reference.

It's important to note that the points listed here are not exhaustive; you may have additional elements to consider when determining the priority of a prospect. Perhaps you're already familiar with the competition and aim to focus on prospects where your competitor is weak.

Now that you've segmented your accounts by size into A-B-C-D groups and initiated the assignment of priorities (High, Medium, Low), you're poised to progress to the establishment of more intricate categories.

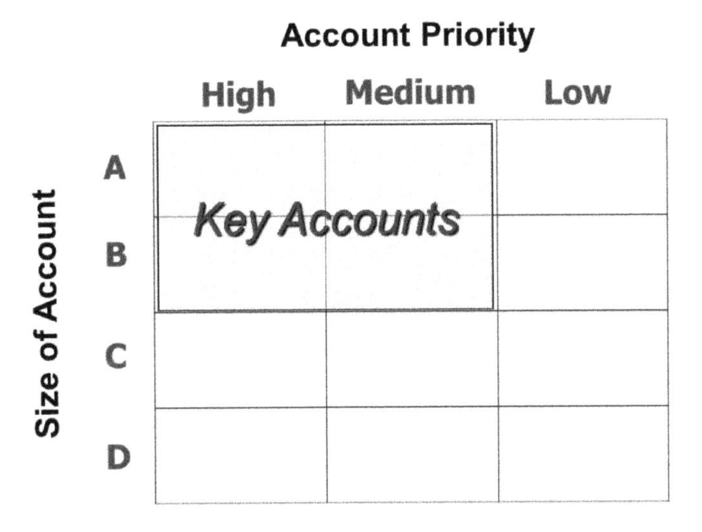

Coverage Requirements

Now that we have discussed segmenting and prioritizing the prospects and customers in your market let's talk about calculating the coverage capability. No salesperson can do it all. You will miss considerable business, opportunity, and market share if you do not have enough resources. So, how much can one salesperson handle? (By the way, there are similar calculations for how many accounts service technicians can cover while maintaining high productivity and customer satisfaction ratings.)

We will use some numbers for illustration, but the calculations are fundamental for you to pay attention to.

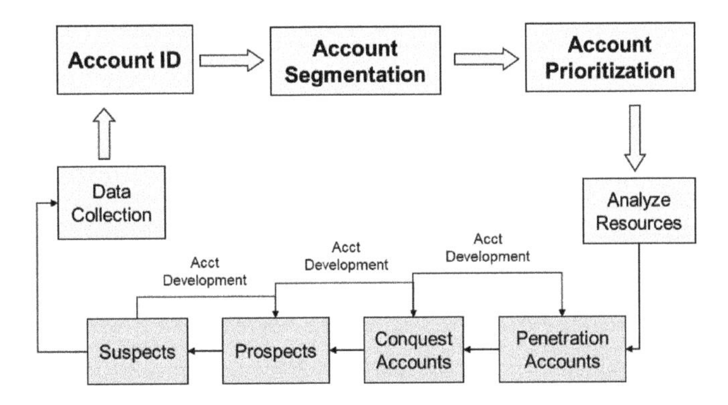

Using the chart above we discussed earlier, we're currently discussing the box on the far right, "Analyze Resources."

We discussed Account Segmentation and Account Prioritization; now, can you handle what is possible?

If one salesperson can deliver $3,000,000 a year in sales and you have eight salespeople, you should see $24,000,000 a year in revenue. If you achieve a 40% market share, you are in a $60,000,000 market.

What do we have to calculate in the other direction? You have a market size of $75,000,000, so how many salespeople do you need, and at what productivity levels?

You will not have every salesperson performing at a fantastic sales level. So you as the sales manager need to do some planning. You probably have some senior salespeople who are experienced and mature and have been with you for several years. You have some new blood who are excited about making money but are not very experienced in handling objections. How do you utilize those people most effectively and give them all room to grow?

Assigned Customer Group

Slsp Experience	Mature	Average	Fresh
Experienced	$ 480,000	$ 360,000	$ 240,000
Average	$ 360,000	$ 240,000	$ 180,000
New	$ 240,000	$ 180,000	$ 120,000

Gross Profit Dollar Contribution by Salesperson
Normal Progression would happen over approx 5 years.

Each of us is unique, and you will need to assess the skills and capabilities of your staff. However, one of the measurements of salespeople is the gross profit they can deliver from their sales efforts for the dealership. Using $240,000 a year in delivered gross profit as a central starting point, we might look at a growth chart like the one above. Notice we are building a matrix between the salesperson's experience and the customer's maturity. Experienced salespeople will have the skills to handle objections, sell higher-value products and services, and deliver better gross profit to the dealership.

Remember, we can't take sales volume or market share to the bank. If we don't have money left from making sales, running this dealership is coming out of someone else's pockets.

Sales management would be easy if we plotted all salespeople on this chart and knew how they would perform. But then, where is the fun in that?

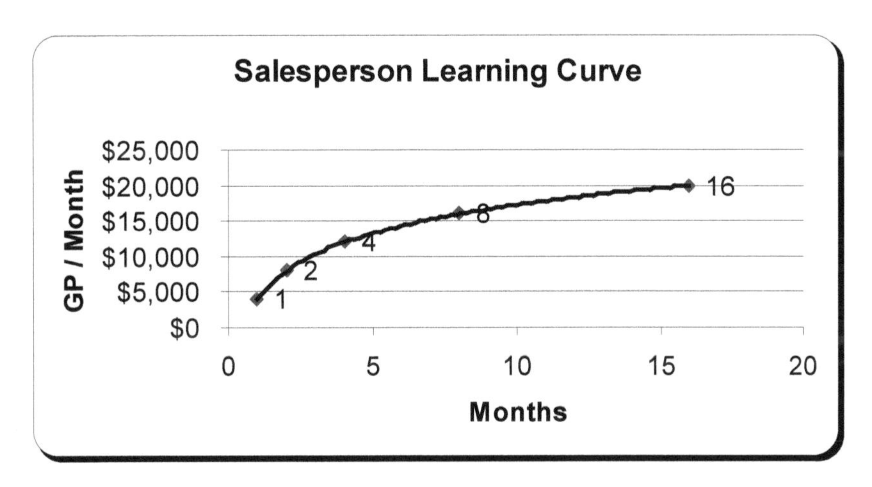

New salespeople should read the books, learn the products quickly, and go out and sell, right? Well, the learning curve is not that linear. Education research has shown that a new person will double their knowledge every two months. So, if they start in month one, they might stumble over business. By the end of month two, they know twice as much more. But they are still not experienced salespeople. It generally takes 16-18 months for a new salesperson to understand what you hired them to do. (This assumes they knew nothing of your business, industry, or sales before. Hiring a salesperson from the competition will have benefits and pitfalls.) Several factors will impact their learning:

1. Product/Service Complexity: If the products or services being sold are complex and require in-depth knowledge, the learning curve may be longer.
2. Sales Cycle Length: The sales cycle length in a particular industry or for a specific product can influence the learning curve. Longer sales cycles may require a more extended period to understand and navigate.
3. The sales cycle for a salesperson was 12-18 months, from finding a prospect to closing a deal.
4. Industry Experience: Prior experience in the industry can significantly reduce the learning curve. Sales professionals with industry knowledge may adapt more quickly.

5. Training and Onboarding: The effectiveness of the sales training and onboarding process is critical. A well-structured program can accelerate learning by providing essential skills, product knowledge, and sales techniques.
6. You should have a template of the items needed for a new salesperson to accomplish and a checklist with dates when those items are accomplished. Reading the sales literature, completing the CRM training program, attending the manufacturer's product training course, etc.
7. Customer Base and Relationships: Building client relationships is often an essential aspect of sales. The time it takes to establish a network and understand the customer base can influence the learning curve.
8. Sales Strategy and Techniques: The adoption and mastery of sales strategies and techniques, such as prospecting, objection handling, and closing deals, contribute to the learning curve.
9. Market Dynamics: Understanding market dynamics, competition, and industry trends is crucial. Sales professionals need time to grasp the nuances of the market they are operating in.
10. Individual Skills and Adaptability: The natural aptitude for sales, communication skills, and adaptability of the individual also play a role. Some individuals may adapt more quickly to the demands of a sales role.

Some salespeople will take advantage of the numbers. They will quote more than other salespeople, and the easy closes float to the top, and they close those deals. Other salespeople will only quote a deal they know they can close. Your challenge is to identify these routines and train those salespeople to be in on more deals and close at a higher percentage.

Making the change from taking orders and selling equipment to acquiring accounts is such a major leap of faith and change in belief that many companies just throw up their hands and admit that they don't have the persistence to make the change. But at least they are honest with themselves.

Acquiring accounts is about creating solutions and not about selling.

In the early days, it was about selling units. Then competition (both from brands and other dealers/distributors) came along, and it became about selling the product cheaper than the other guy; but as the Evolution of the Market continues and the customers start entering the "Total Cost of Ownership" phase of purchasing they are looking for complete packages that deliver solutions. These solutions bring together the quality product, the focus and intelligence of you, the dealer, to maintain the equipment for minimum downtime, repair cost, and maximum value for as long as reasonable, and then turn this product over for a new replacement.

Account Management is just that, managing the account with solutions so the customer sees constant value from you. They see enough value that they pay you not only the value of the product and service but also a premium for the added value of your knowledge.

When you begin to think about customer solutions, changes to the customer's industry, the impact that will have on the customer, and what you can provide in new and enhanced solutions, you are beginning to manage accounts and not sales.

When the prospect calls and says, "I want one of those xxxxx things!" Does the person on the other end of the phone say, "Well, those are very nice, but let's talk about your company and what solutions you need and are looking for?" Or do they ask, "How soon do you want it delivered?" The first person is possibly more concerned about the customer's total solution. (Of course, if they were just out of stock and trying to substitute another product, that is not really caring about the customer.)

When the prospect or customer calls and reaches someone in parts, does the parts person take enough time to find out the customer's problem (or pain) to suggest the correct solution in the company, or do they take down part numbers and ship them?

Account management is where the dealership people start caring about customer solutions and see profitable solutions they can create, sell, or provide to the customer instead of just how many units the customer will buy. A salesperson may go to a customer site and talk about replacement sales of equipment, but another salesperson may go and see significant parts and labor business that will bring more profits and satisfy the customer at less capital investment. The second salesperson may create a better relationship with the customer and sell more units later.

Account management is about relationships, the long-term revenue stream, solutions, and acquiring all of the customers' businesses.

This takes vision, selflessness, faith, and dedication. This is not about how to get a commission on this deal in the next 30 days because that will pay for the new patio or kids' school fees.

We will deal with many of these issues in the Recruiting and Training Chapter.

7. Managing the Sales Force

Expectations of Salespeople & Sales Department Staff

All salespeople sell better as they get more experience, right? Then look at the chart below!

Rank	Industry	Count of Source	% of Slsm	Average of Revenue	Average of Gross Profit$	Average of GP %	Average of Years of Industry Experience
A	Ag	3	0.26%	$5,712,380	$767,736	14.07%	8
	Const	137	11.66%	$6,454,628	$1,004,110	22.59%	12
	Lift	2	0.17%	$4,301,723	$806,419	19.69%	23
A Total		**142**	**12.09%**	**$6,408,624**	**$996,331**	**22.37%**	**12**
B	Ag	30	2.55%	$3,962,896	$365,892	10.75%	18
	Const	217	18.47%	$3,150,547	$408,427	16.22%	10
	Lift	11	0.94%	$2,174,111	$371,591	18.94%	13
	Tire	7	0.60%	$1,518,408	$315,999	21.85%	17
B Total		**265**	**22.55%**	**$3,158,867**	**$399,641**	**15.86%**	**11**
C	Ag	94	8.00%	$2,317,160	$200,259	10.24%	15
	Const	175	14.89%	$1,665,829	$211,850	14.71%	12
	Lift	54	4.60%	$1,484,192	$196,809	14.83%	12
	Tire	21	1.79%	$1,011,901	$210,491	22.41%	11
C Total		**344**	**29.28%**	**$1,775,376**	**$206,239**	**13.98%**	**13**
D	Ag	122	10.38%	$1,026,146	$88,700	10.15%	10
	Comp	23	1.96%	$315,767	$64,849	21.02%	13
	Const	99	8.43%	$764,739	$88,250	13.28%	7
	Lift	147	12.51%	$641,567	$79,726	13.96%	10
	Tire	33	2.81%	$589,136	$92,801	17.37%	15
D Total		**424**	**36.09%**	**$759,230**	**$84,509**	**13.36%**	**10**
Grand Total		1175	100.00%	$2,280,653	$301,414	15.19%	11

This chart ranked salespeople in various industries according to the gross profit they delivered to the dealership. The sales volume, pricing, and gross profit in each industry are different, but here we ranked salespeople who brought the top 40% of the gross profit as "A Salespeople"; salespeople who brought the next 30% were "B Salespeople"; the next 20% delivered became the "C Salespeople," and the last 10% of Gross Profit was the "D Salespeople."

As you look over this chart of real information from each of these industries, you'll notice that the number of years of experience is not very different in each category. You'll also notice that the gross profit percentage can go up or down from one group to the other within an industry, but the real difference is how much gross profit money the salespeople in that segment deliver. Since we discussed the impact of medical coverage and commission, you can see what this will mean to the dealership.

One of the most critical determinants of salespeople's productivity is the total dollars of gross profit they deliver. Of course, your job as a sales manager is to hold them to this volume of gross profit and maintain the quality of sales calls and the quality of the gross profit margin.

Productivity

You must analyze productivity to ensure that your sales department meets the expectations defined in the Financial Model and specifically in the Sales Department Model. Such an analysis helps you identify how your department is performing in relation to goals and how to improve that performance.

Methods Of Analyzing Productivity

There are two basic methods of analyzing productivity, each with its own measure:

- Departmental-Measured by the market share your company is capturing in its market area.
- Individual-Measured by the Gross Profit contribution per salesperson.

Departmental Productivity

Analyzing your participation and closure rates in your market area would be best to meet your market share expectations. By examining and measuring participation and closure, you can identify possible methods of achieving the benchmark defined in the Financial Model.

Benchmark = XX% Market Share

Participation

Participation measures how well your salespeople are blanketing your market area. Your participation figure indicates the percentage of the available business you compete on.

Are you calling on and competing for 50 percent of the available business in the market area or are you competing for 90 percent?

Because each purchase's unit sales volume may differ, your participation percentage must be based on dollars of equipment sold, not on the number of sales agreements. Therefore, the participation figure is a weighted number based on dollars.

To calculate participation, you must know how many dollars or units of new and used equipment in your market area are purchased yearly. Your participation is the percentage of those dollars for which you competed.

Closure

Closure is a measure of your success in selling to fleets. It analyzes how effectively and successfully your salespeople present your Package Of Value. Closure is the percentage of orders you receive divided by the quotations you make.

To determine your closure rate, you must keep a log of quotations and update the log so you can determine which quotations are converted to sales. For more information about quote logs, refer to Chapter 15.

Orders ÷ Quotations = Closure Rate

Market Share

You get market share if you multiply your participation rate times your closure rate.

Participation Rate x Closure Rate = Market Share

Suppose your salespeople are calling on and competing for 80 percent of the business in the market (participation) and selling 60 percent of the business they compete on (closure). In that case, your market share is 48 percent.

Participation	Closure	Market Share
80%	60%	48%
50%	50%	25%
75%	60%	45%
30%	100%	30%
80%	80%	64%
90%	80%	72%

You must have participation and closure because you want to increase your market share. The analysis of participation and closure helps you analyze opportunities for improvement.

If your participation rate is low, you must determine how to help your salespeople present to more fleets. If your participation rate is high but your closure rate is low, you must help your salespeople sell more effectively.

Problem: Low Participation

A low participation rate indicates your salespeople aren't calling on enough fleets. There are several possible reasons.

Too few salespeople.

Refer to Chapter 12 to learn more about analyzing your sales capacity in your market area.

Salespeople are making too few calls.

This may be due to a lack of motivation or wasted time because of poor time management.

Salespeople are not calling on the correct accounts.

This may be due to poor account prioritization or a failure to observe the assigned call frequency for target accounts.

Salespeople are not actively competing for available business.

This would indicate that salespeople are making the correct number of calls to the proper accounts but are not allowed to make quotes or presentations.

You must achieve high participation in your market area to implement your sales plan effectively. If your participation is currently low, refer to the chapters mentioned above to help you find the solution to this problem.

Problem: Low Closure

If your closure rate is low, your salespeople aren't selling effectively. There are several possible reasons.

1. The Package of Value is not aligned with fleet needs. Learn more about fleet needs and the Package Of Value
2. Salespeople lack sales skills. The most effective way for them to learn sales skills and product knowledge is through a program. However, sales skills alone are not enough. You must also coach your salespeople to help them develop and adequately use those skills.
3. Salespeople lack persuasive selling tools or do not know how to use them effectively.

To implement your sales plan effectively, you must achieve high closure in your market area. If your closure is currently low, refer to the chapters and resources mentioned above to help you find the solution to this problem.

Individual Productivity

Whether your departmental productivity is on target or not, you must analyze productivity individually. An individual analysis helps you identify personal opportunities for members of your sales team to make improvements.

To measure individual productivity, you must calculate the Gross Profit contribution of each sales team member.

Then, compare the amount of each Gross Profit contribution to the individual's quota/sales goal.

When determining an individual's quota, consider that salesperson's experience and history and the benchmark defined in the Wise Wolf Consulting' Financial Model.

Benchmark = $240,000 Gross Profit Per Salesperson

This financial benchmark is calculated as a department average. Therefore, it is possible to have some salespeople with a Gross Profit contribution higher than $240,000 and others with a Gross Profit contribution lower than $240,000 and still achieve the benchmark. However, it would help if you strived to create a sales team in which every member meets or surpasses this benchmark.

Problem: Sales Below Quota

When your salespeople fail to meet quota, you must identify the reasons for failure and help them become more effective. There are two primary reasons for failing to meet an individual sales goal:

1. The salesperson is not making the required sales calls. This may be due to a lack of motivation or poor time management.
2. The salesperson is not making effective sales calls. There are numerous reasons for ineffective sales calls. The salesperson may not be talking to the right people or asking the right questions. It is also possible that the salesperson is not be presenting the Package Of Value appropriately. The Fleet Selling Process, included in this module, can assist you in coaching such problems.

Once you have identified the primary reason for a salesperson's low productivity, you can work with the individual to determine the specific factors contributing to the problem.

Then, together, you and your employee can agree on action steps that they can take to improve their performance.

What do you expect from each position

Sales Manager Talents

- Manage their salespeople effectively
- Motivate their salespeople
- Collect and Analyze competitive data to evaluate the markets
- Develop Sales Strategies
- Recruit Top Salespeople
- Direct efforts and resources effectively and efficiently
- Utilize a database in marketing efforts

We recommend the dealer principal share his evaluation with the sales manager. Rate each skill listed using the rating scale shown on the form in Chapter 10. A brief description of those skills unique to the sales manager follows.

Competitive Analysis

Understand each competitor's strengths, weaknesses, and marketing strategy. Uses this knowledge to develop the dealer's marketing strategy. Able to anticipate competitive responses to dealer's marketing initiatives.

Motivation

Understand and apply the factors impacting the sales performance of each salesperson (e.g., money, recognition, challenging accounts, etc.). Creates a working environment conducive to meeting these driving forces.

Recruiting

Understand basic interviewing techniques and apply these when recruiting personnel. Identifies and hires high performing salespersonnel.

Evaluating Performance

Periodically reviews performance of each salesperson using objective standards (e.g., close ratio, market share, profit margin, account coverage, etc...). Develops, in conjunction with each salesperson, action plans to improve performance.

Coaching

Provides council and guidance to sales force. Actively works with salespersonnel to improve sales techniques and performance consistant.

Developing Compensation Programs

Understands and applies various options available for sales compensation. Selects programs that maximize benefits to salespersonnel and dealership alike.

Marketing

Uses database marketing, telemarketing, advertising, direct mail and sales promotion to develop dealer awareness and support dealer sales efforts

Statistical Analysis

Understands, computes and applies various statistical measures to manage sales activity (i.e. market share, awareness, closure, call ratios, etc.).

Training

Identifies personnel performance deficiencies and develops training programs to correct these deficiencies.

Territory Management Account Assignment

Sizes territories based upon sales opportunity and prospect demographics. Uses a formal process to manage salespersonnel call performance and quote activity

Your Training Program Outline:

1. **Take the Lead** - stresses the importance of the salesperson's presence in the sales relationship.
2. **Invest in the Relationship** - see the customer problems as the customer does, develop long-term relationships.
3. **Get Organized** - maximize selling time, have concrete objectives/strategies for sales calls, coaching by sales managers.
4. **Find the Area of Opportunity** - master a method for determining client needs by asking the right questions.
5. **Present with a Purpose** - assume winning attitude, uncover/respond to hidden objections, remain organized.
6. **Make Customer Part of Solution** - emphasize benefit of your product to customer and recognize buying signals.
7. **Close for Results** - know when to close, use right close, deliver with confidence.
8. **Assume the Responsibility** - enhance long-term relationships, shorten sales-cycles, insulate competitive activity.
9. **Become the Only Choice** - respond to the challenge of "So what? Now what?" Develop concrete action plans.
10. **Negotiations** - master the give & take, never give without getting something back.

Salesperson Talents

Your training of Salespeople should lead to your dealership benefiting.

- Greatly expand business in existing accounts - Increase in sales/profits
- Reopen lost accounts - Reducing the turnover in your sales force.
- Revitalize marginal accounts - Increasing teamwork and cooperation.
- Confidently call on new accounts - Rapidly developing new business.
- Capture accounts from competition - Quickly reach your sales objectives.
- Improve your position in all accounts - Expanding your market share long-term

Recommended Skills

While these are some general skills to consider you might want to add others.

We recommend assessing the skill levels for your salespeople on at least an annual basis, and identifying training or skill building activities for those that need improvement.

Organization

Formulates long- and short-range plans that are significant and measurable. Plans sales tasks and projects effectively. Administration of paperwork is current and accurate.

Communications

Maintains clear internal and external personal lines of communications. Can easily articulate and transfer ideas to customers, peers and management.

Decision Making

Gathers information independently and makes quality decisions based upon the analysis. Able to provide justification of decisions and courses of action.

Handling Emergencies

Handles unexpected problems/demands to the best advantage of organization. Has the ability to prioritize customer special requests. Works well under pressure.

Professionalism

Consistently maintains a positive attitude, image and demeanor befitting a professional. Actively pursues the growth of the business.

Self-Development

Sets self-improvement goals. Seeks out and utilizes feedback from direct management and peers. Seems to know own strengths and weaknesses and strives to improve performance.

Dealing With Other Departments

Works effectively with other people in the company.

Managing Company Funds

Makes economic decisions that best utilize assets such as demos, expense and budgetary dollars.

Performance

Consistently meets annual sales objectives. Do not rate the salesperson based on their current sales numbers versus quota, instead consider whether or not this person is a reliable contributor to the goals of the dealership.

Listening

Is attentive to the speaker and uses non-verbal communication skills (e.g. eye contact, standing attentively) while listening. Does not interrupt others as they are speaking. Does not jump to conclusions. Attempts to uncover speaker's message by asking appropriate questions and requests clarification when necessary.

Telephone Techniques

Speaks in a friendly but businesslike manner. Does not perform other activities during call, i.e. all efforts are concentrated on what caller is saying. Returns calls in a timely manner.

Letter and Proposal writing

Writes clearly and concisely, providing complete information. Can express how your company's products and services can meet specific customer requirements.

Selling Skills

Understanding a variety of buyer types. Use good questioning skills and then present solutions professionally that effectively closes the customer's gap.

Competitive Analysis

Understands each competitor's strengths, weaknesses and marketing strategy.

Knows when and how to use this information to maximum advantage during sales calls, the proposal process and demonstrations.

Financial Merchandising

Has a working knowledge of various financial merchandising alternatives. These include true leases, conditional sales contracts, full payment leases, long term rental, and Fleet programs. Actively quotes financial alternatives where appropriate.

Maintenance Contracts

Has a working knowledge of available maintenance contracts. Actively promotes concept of maintenance contracts where appropriate.

Equipment Demos

Actively utilizes demos as a selling technique. Has the ability to highlight your product features and benefits that relate to the customer's specific requirements during a walk around.

Negotiating

Demonstrates good negotiating skills. Anticipates and prepares for a Fair Exchange. Has the ability to alleviate customer concerns by illustrating value-added benefits gained by doing business with the your dealership and selling your products.

Presentations

Conveys message to customer in a clear and concise manner consistent with the professional selling skills in the your training program. Message is targeted at specific customer needs. Uses visual aids to reinforce key points.

Prospecting

Has good understanding of equipment customer demographics and is able to use this knowledge to identify potential prospects via telephone or cold calls. Follows up on sales leads in a timely manner.

Territory Management

Accounts are prioritized as A, B, C or D. Plans call frequency based upon prioritization. Effectively uses telephone in conjunction with sales calls to maintain contact with customer. Maintains up to date information on account demographics.

Product Knowledge and Application

Has a working knowledge of equipment performance characteristics, associated with each product type (e.g., drive lines, electric power, engine power and hydraulics, etc.). Understands how each product is used in various material handling applications (e.g., order picking, shipping, receiving, production, etc.).

Attachment Knowledge and Application

Has a working knowledge of attachment offerings, applications, and benefits of use. Understands the effect of an installed attachment on equipment performance.

Application Surveys

Able to conduct application survey at customer location to determine material handling requirements. Actively recommends performing an application survey during the proposal process.

Fuel Sources

Has working knowledge of equipment power sources, gasoline, diesel, propane, batteries, and charger functions and how they relate to equipment performance. Has the ability to select the source for the application based upon the analysis of key factors such as the duty cycle, environmental conditions, and cost benefits.

Organizing Territories, Assignments, and Teams

The Art of Strategic Sales Resource Allocation

Imagine yourself as a conductor leading an orchestra.

Your instruments are your salespeople, and your score is your sales strategy. Each salesperson possesses unique strengths and talents; your task is to orchestrate their efforts for maximum impact. This requires a deep understanding of resource allocation, a critical skill for any sales manager.

Segment	Percentage of Business	Number of Calls/ Yr	# of Calls Per Year	Number of Accounts
A	40%	400	24	17
B	30%	300	12	25
C	20%	200	4	50
D	10%	100	1	100
Total	100%	1,000		192

The above chart looks at how many calls we expect can be accomplished in the year, then allocating them by segment or size of accounts for more frequent to large or complex accounts and less frequent to smaller accounts. Remember that if the larger accounts have more units and more opportunities to sell more units, they deliver more money in sales and gross profit dollars. So, we are expecting the salespeople to spend more time there. We might even look at the above chart and ask why we would spend 100 calls on the small accounts if they could be covered in another way, such as flyers, brochures, outbound calls, etc.

Your salespeople are your most valuable resource, and their time is their most valuable asset. Just like a service technician's productivity is measured by their hourly output, a salesperson's success often hinges on the number of calls they can make. While the number of calls varies across industries, understanding this metric is crucial for effective resource allocation.

Not all accounts are created equal. Some, like the "A Accounts", represent a significant portion of your business and require more frequent contact. Others, like the "D Accounts", may be better served by alternative methods like flyers or outbound calls. The key lies in segmenting your accounts based on size, profitability, and potential value and allocating calls accordingly.

Don't forget to bring prospects and customer accounts to each salesperson's total accounts. You might balance the accounts 1/3 prospects and 2/3 customers, or ½ customer and ½ prospects; it will depend on your sales strategy for the salespeople and what your company needs.

From the illustration above, you should be able to see what would happen to a salesperson with 500 assigned accounts. If the chart shows what they can accomplish with balanced coverage based on the size of the accounts, at least 300 accounts in that 500 would not be covered, called on, or approached in the next year. Why waste your breath complaining to the salesperson about what they "are not accomplishing" when, according to the chart, they could not cover

Territory vs. Account Assignment

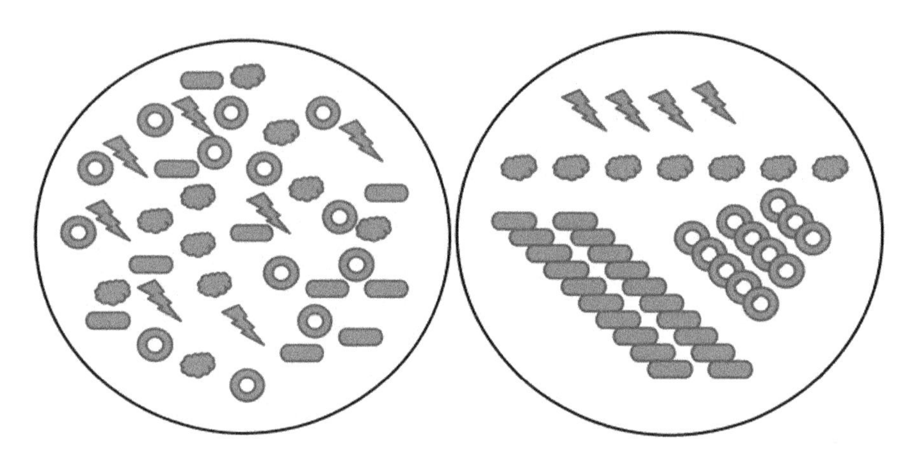

What's wrong with having geographic "territories?" Nothing! The point is that "territories" generally indicate a style and philosophy that says sales managers have "abdicated," "delegated," or "abandoned" the function of determining who and how salespeople will organize, structure, and work their group of accounts. When we use the term "account assignment," we are talking about a group of specific accounts (by name) that are assigned to a salesperson, and the salesperson is "responsible and accountable" for demonstrating results. Sometimes, the salesperson has a "territory" like the circle illustrated here. What's wrong with this "territory?" There is no plan for it. There is no expectation of results and coverage. When the salesperson achieves the sales goal, is it because they worked all the accounts or just part of them? Are they getting as much out of the accounts as possible? What is the potential?

What is different about the accounts represented in the next circle? Well, here we know how many of each type of account there are, possibly what the potential business is, and what "accountable" behavior looks like in covering these accounts.

Yes, the first group of accounts in the territory could be organized and "cleaned up," but our experience is that there is a mindset difference. In the first approach, the salesperson is "entitled" to all the business within the geography. This is not because they call on or work these accounts but because they are "entitled" to what comes out of the geography because that is what they were given, charged with, or held accountable for from the beginning.

In the second example, the salesperson was given a list of accounts with names and addresses.

It did not matter if these accounts were geographically organized; they were a list of accounts on a set of pages, and that is what they were given, charged with or held accountable. The mindset is different!

When a prospect with the same county or zip code calls and wants to buy your product, they don't immediately expect the commission. Why should they receive a commission if they didn't call on the account or find them? And if they are calling on the accounts assigned to them, how did they "find" this account? Do you see the logic? It's pretty obvious!

The final point is that this is not impossible; it just requires someone to make real decisions, watch the results, and adjust to the future as things progress.

A Team Approach to Account Coverage

Mature account management frequently involves more than one salesperson to one account. Consider your absolute number one customer, are you comfortable leaving your business relationship with that account in the hands of one single salesperson? What would happen if that salesperson left, went to the competition, or went to work for that large customer?

If you have high Priority "A" Level accounts, you might seriously consider having a team involved with those accounts. Consider a multi-frequency schedule of salespeople and managers' involvement. The team Schedule might look like:

Dealer Principal	Twice a Year
Senior Management	Quarterly Visits
Equipment Salesperson	Twice a Month
Aftermarket Salesperson	Twice a Month

Initially, some people look at a schedule like this and say that is too much coverage for one account. But if that account is 2-5% of your business, can you afford to not be in their business that frequently?

A-High Existing	A-High Conquest	A-Medium Existing	A-Medium Conquest
DLR Prin – 2 Sr. Mgmt Team – 4 Unit Sales Rep – 24 A/M Sales Rep - 24	DLR Prin – 3 Sr Mgmt Team – 6 Unit Sales Rep -18 A/M Sales Rep – 12	DLR Prin – 1 Sr Mgmt Team – 2 Unit Sales Rep -24 A/M Sales Rep – 24	DLR Prin – 2 Sr Mgmt Team – 4 Unit Sales Rep -12 A/M Sales Rep – 12

B-High Conquest	C-High Existing	C-Medium Existing	D-High Existing
DLR Prin – 1 Sr. Mgmt Team – 3 Unit Sales Rep – 12 A/M Sales Rep – 6	DLR Prin – 0 Sr Mgmt Team – 1 Unit Sales Rep -4 A/M Sales Rep – 2 Telemarketing - 12	DLR Prin – 0 Sr Mgmt Team – 0 Unit Sales Rep -4 A/M Sales Rep – 2 Telemarketing - 12	DLR Prin – 0 Sr Mgmt Team – 0 Unit Sales Rep -1 A/M Sales Rep – 0 Telemarketing – 6 Technician - 12

The charts above highlight the inclusion of Conquest accounts, representing prospects with high potential for conversion into valuable customers. Account Management extends beyond merely managing existing customers; it encompasses the strategic cultivation of prospects. Dedicating time and effort to nurturing these relationships is crucial for expanding your customer base and achieving sustainable growth. Ignoring Conquest accounts essentially forfeits the opportunity to acquire their business and unlock their potential value.

The two charts above illustrate what you might do to organize your sales efforts to include a blend of customers and prospects.

Developing Your Target Customer Philosophy

Many choices are possible; what you do with them is part of your company's package of value and what will make you unique. Do you want to address selling "competitively priced products," "quality merchandise," or "cost of ownership," to name a few? These grand strategy decisions show that companies will be more receptive or less receptive to your style, influencing who you target.

8. Account Management

Current Accounts

Your target customer philosophy applies to existing accounts and the new accounts you target. As you develop your target customer philosophy, you should consider your existing accounts and develop strategies for account retention and penetration.

Account retention is keeping customers you already have. Account penetration is selling more of your products and services to existing customers.

Account Retention

Gaining an account demands a considerable amount of effort and resources. Keeping good accounts is far more profitable than constantly seeking to gain new ones. This is due to the transparent costs associated with serving existing customers, in contrast to the unpredictable costs of acquiring and catering to new customers. However, it's important to recognize that not all existing customers are beneficial to serve. You might find that some of your current customers are not worth the effort. A key aspect of your sales management strategy should be to regularly evaluate the profitability of each account, considering sales, gross profit, and expenses. This evaluation helps in guiding your sales team effectively, showing them where to focus their efforts. Above all, the retention of valuable accounts is vital for your company's success, making it a top strategic priority.

Account Penetration

When examining your existing accounts, it's likely that you'll find that 80 percent of your business comes from just 20 percent of your clients. It's probable that this key 20 percent have the capacity to purchase even more from you. There's usually room to increase sales of your current products or services they're already buying, or they might be interested in other products or services that they haven't purchased from you yet. This process is essentially what we mean by account penetration.

Why put effort into pursuing new clients when there's a wealth of unrealized potential within the customer base you already have?

Category Segmentation

You can categorize accounts according to relationship type. These categories refer to what you know about them and your current business relationship. Knowing the category they fit allows you to plan your strategy with them. There are four account categories:

- **Existing Accounts.** Existing accounts are your customers, but they may offer significant potential for additional business.
- **Conquest Accounts.** Conquest accounts are those fleets that aren't currently buying from you but have high volume and profit potential.
- **Prospect Accounts**. Prospect accounts are fleets you may not know much about currently, but your data about those fleets suggests they may offer significant volume and profit potential.
- **Suspect Accounts.** Suspect accounts are just fleet names you've discovered while gathering information for your market area.

Difference between Territory Coverage and Account Coverage

In the early days of manufacturers selling through dealers or distributors, their concern was to cover the geography so that someone was responsible for the state, county, or geographic area. Then, hold that organization accountable for the results. If they could not accomplish what was expected, then find someone else.

Similarly, in the early days of the dealership or distributor, the process was to find a salesperson to put in charge of the geography and make them accountable for results. In this fashion, the dealer/distributor expected the salesperson to "manage the accounts" within the geography. Some salespeople found the top accounts and did an outstanding job of this. Others found enough business to keep their supervisor or manufacturer happy. But in many (if not most) cases, the significant opportunity was missed, ignored, or passed up. So long as enough results occurred, no one looked for more.

The crucial question of the market's potential within a defined geographical area was rarely, if ever, asked, explored, or considered.

The approach of "Account Management" is to analyze the potential of the accounts and assign enough accounts to a salesperson that you can permeate the accounts for equipment sales, market share and penetrate the aftermarket potential of the accounts.

Assigning too many accounts to a salesperson means they cannot cover all of them. Assigning too few means they cannot reach their potential. You are the sales manager and are responsible for determining the correct assignment and coverage. You need to assign your resources (salespeople and their time) in such a way that you maximize your assets for optimal coverage and sales results.

Segmenting Accounts

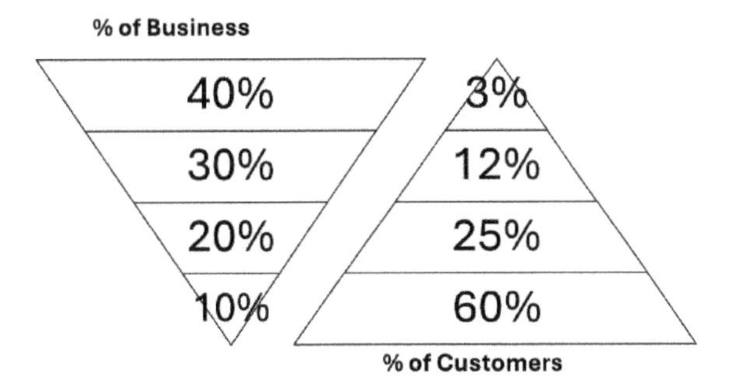

One way to know how to assign your resources correctly is to segment your accounts so that you can assign resources to the most significant portion of your business. We discussed some of this earlier in the book. Run your descending sales report (the more history you can include in the report, the more stable the results will be for you). Of course, you need to process some things in the list, like what transactions are for finance companies, cash accounts, internal transactions, multiple ship-tos for specific accounts, and what accounts have gone out of business since those sales.

Grouping the business now by 40%-30%-20% & 10% will group them into what we generally name the A-B-C-D segments. These are merely organized by size or volume purchasing. We are including equipment, parts, service, and rental purchases in the descending report here.

Profiling From Segmentation

Segment	% of Business	Number of Units
A	40%	26+
B	30%	11 - 25
C	20%	4 – 10
D	10%	1 – 3

Now, you can start to use the data! From what you have done, look at just the "A Accounts". In some industries, we have found some unique aspects of the accounts standards that we can identify for the group of accounts. Interestingly, in three industries we work in, the consistent feature of these accounts is that they own or use a certain number of equipment units.

While this consistent feature works in construction, forklifts, and agricultural equipment, it will not always work in other industries like air compressors, golf carts or generators. In those industries, the amount of consumption is more critical to the account than the number of units used to accomplish it.

But by finding this profiling characteristic from the organization of the accounts, you can begin to identify the potential of the accounts each salesperson is responsible for. So when you see substantial variances between salespeople's number of accounts and their potential, you can begin to balance opportunity or improve coverage.

Salesperson	Number of Accounts	Potential Units	Market Share	Units Sold per Year
# 1	185	2,077	10.2%	212
# 2	423	3,988	5.1%	205
# 3	511	5,647	3.5%	198

While the chart above may be extreme, it is intended to illustrate that salespeople often bring in about the same number of unit sales no matter the number of accounts they cover. Sometimes, they don't cover some accounts because of time limitations or previous relationships. It would be interesting to analyze the three salespeople above and see which accounts were called on and worked and which were never called on or contacted. The results could be that they all called on the same 185 accounts to accomplish their final results. If that was the case, what happened to the other accounts in the salespersons #2 and #3 situation? There was no coverage there! So what should you do? Hire other salespeople or chastise the existing salespeople for not covering the accounts?

Who's job is it to accomplish the assignment and the coverage of accounts? Yours or theirs? Who is the manager?

Identifying Fleets or Pivotal Accounts

In each industry, geography, and business, there are pivotal accounts that the dealership/distributor has built important relationships with and developed strong relationships with. You must look at these strategically. What is the importance of your company to them, and what is the importance of their business to you?

A good strategy will drive you to build stronger relationships between your two companies. Monthly or quarterly reviews might be an obvious need, and they also keep you in touch with these accounts. It is probably a group of accounts that you have senior salespeople involved in, but you should probably include other senior management from your company with theirs. The broader and more profound the ties, the better for you.

Prioritizing Accounts

You know that all fleets in your market area can be segmented by size, and the largest fleets offer the most tremendous potential for sales volume and profitability.

You also know that not all fleets-large or small-offer the same potential. Some will be Phase II buyers, focused only on the initial price. Some will have poor credit ratings. Some will want Packages Of Value you can't provide.

Because your potential return from each fleet differs, you must analyze and prioritize them. This analysis will lead you to select the fleets that offer the most potential as target accounts.

Priority Segmentation

After size segmentation, the next level of segmentation involves analyzing and identifying priority. You can prioritize your accounts as high, medium, or low priority.

As the sales manager, you are responsible for deciding what makes a high, medium or low-priority account. Here are some criteria you can use to identify your high-priority accounts:

- You already have an established relationship with the fleet.
- The fleet buys in Phase II or Phase N
- The fleet's location is near your business.
- The fleet pays on time.
- The fleet is logistically easy to service.
- The fleet has an annual growth rate of 20 percent or more.
- The fleet has adequate capitalization.

On the other hand, if a fleet is declining in size, buys in Phase II, has shrinking capitalization, pays in 90 days, is challenging to do business with, and is 150 miles away, you would probably assign it a low-priority status.

You must decide how to assign priority to accounts in your market area. Then, you must analyze each fleet and determine its overall priority for your business. Once you've done that, you can select target accounts.

This sample Priority Rating Form illustrates what you might create in your company to account for the various elements that impact your priorities.

Using just one of the various priority elements above, let's illustrate what might happen to the accounts in each segment.

Sample Illustration of Priority Rating System

Market Phase	
Outsource	4
Ownership	3
Price	1
Product	2
Unknown	0

Profit %	
0	1
10%	2
15%	3
20%	4

Growth	
Declining	-1
Flat	1
High	4
Low	2
Medium	3

Relationship	
Average	2
Cool	1
Strong	3

Industry	
Cotton	1
Dairy	1
Hay	2
Lifestyle	3
Orchard	2
Other	0
Rice	1
Row Crops	2
Specialty	4
Vineyard	4

Brand	
Agco	4
Case	3
Caterpillar	2
Deere	3
Ditch Witch	1
Komatsu	1
Kubota	2
Massey	4
New Hollar	3
Vermeer	1

Units	
0	1
4	2
11	3
26	4

Location	
Close	3
Far	1
Medium	2

Ranking	
0.01	D
2.25	C
2.75	B
3.25	A

Listing is in Alphabetic Secquence for Lookup Purposes

	Priority		
Segments	**High**	**Medium**	**Low**
A – 40%			
B – 30%			
C – 20%			
D – 10%			

If in the above chart, "High Priority" was the account being close to the company, "Medium" was 50 miles away, and "Low Priority" was over 100 miles away, then you probably would want to focus on the "high priority" accounts in the A & B segments. But you might decide that the amount of business in the "medium priority A accounts" is so big that you would focus there before going to the "High Priority C Accounts." So, the focus would be from the top left down to the bottom right.

The same approach could be used on how well the accounts pay their bills and their approach to the brands they like, but the ranking of priorities for each account will not always be the same. Some accounts might pay their bills well and prefer your brand equipment but be more than 100 miles away. Other accounts could be close; prefer your brand but not pay their bills quickly. So you have to prioritize these priority elements and then total them up.

Account	Segment	Distance	Credit	Brand	Total Priority
# 42	A	50 = 2	Good = 1	Ours = 1	Total = 4
# 554	A	50 = 2	Fair =2	Mixed = 2	Total = 6
# 756	B	50 =2	Poor =3	Ours = 1	Total = 6
# 866	B	100 =3	Fair =2	Mixed = 2	Total = 7

From the small illustration above you can begin to see that some accounts which have the same size could be more important than others. In this illustration the lower the number for priority the higher the priority of the account. Therefore, #42 is an A Account with a priority ranking of 4, while account #554 is also an A Account but scored 6 in priority; they tend to buy multiple brands, not just ours and they only pay their bills fairly! Think of doing this for all the accounts of a salesperson and then determining where you want to place the strongest effort of the salesperson.

Assigning Resources

Salespeople are your primary resource to create the sales you are responsible for accomplishing. Like service technicians the most significant element they have is their time and what they do with it. In most dealerships the service technicians are measured on their hourly productivity.

Salespeople have this time also, but we generally look at it in the number of calls they can accomplish in a day (or year). In some industries salespeople can accomplish one to two sales calls, in other industries they can achieve four to six calls.

If we considered a salesperson to make 5 calls a day, and only expect them in the field (or following up on call activities four days a week) and give them two weeks of vacation; then we have 5 calls time four days time 50 weeks which will equal 1,000 calls a year.

So if a salesperson could make 1,000 calls a year, where should you assign those 1,000 calls per salesperson to achieve the most return on their time?

Segment	Percentage of Business	Number of Calls/ Yr	# of Calls Per Year	Number of Accounts
A	40%	400	24	17
B	30%	300	12	25
C	20%	200	4	50
D	10%	100	1	100
Total	100%	1,000		192

The above chart is looking first at how many calls we expect can be accomplished in the year, then allocating them by segment or size of accounts for more frequency to large or complex accounts and less frequent to smaller accounts. Remember that if the larger accounts have more units, more opportunity to sell more units they deliver more money in sales and gross profit dollars. So we are expecting the salespeople to spend more time there. In fact, we might even look at the above chart and ask why we would spend 100 calls on the small accounts if they could be covered in another way such as flyers, brochures, out bound calls, etc.

Don't forget to bring prospects as well as customer accounts in the total accounts for each salesperson. You might balance the accounts 1/3 prospects and 2/3 customers, or ½ customer and ½ prospects, it will depend on your sales strategy for the salespeople and what your company needs.

From the illustration you should be able to see what would happen to a salesperson with 500 accounts. If the chart is what they can accomplish with balanced coverage based on the size of the accounts, there are at least 300 accounts in that 500 that would not be covered, called on or approached in the next year. Why waste your breath complaining to the salesperson about what they "are not accomplishing" when according to the chart they could not cover those accounts anyway?

Just taking a break, let's look at this process a little differently:

Territory Management vs. Account Management

Assigning a salesperson to a territory encompassing three counties and 634 customers and prospects can quickly become overwhelming. It's inevitable that they will prioritize their visits based on the time required and the anticipated outcomes, narrowing down their focus to a manageable number of accounts. Overburdening your sales team with an unmanageable workload can lead to frustration for both the salesperson and management.

To mitigate this, we advocate for a strategic restructuring towards an account-based approach for all dealership sales and service activities. This strategy entails designating each account to a specific sales representative, along with other revenue contributors in parts and service departments, optimizing their limited time. By centering your approach around account management, you not only prioritize customer needs but also streamline the time management of your essential personnel. We have observed that for farm equipment dealers, transitioning to this account management structure is one of the most effective strategies to enhance top-line revenue.

Segmenting Accounts

This methodology marks a paradigm shift for many dealerships, inviting a fresh perspective. Begin by expanding your vision beyond your existing clientele; compile a comprehensive list of all potential and current customers within your designated territory. The foundation of enhanced coverage is a thorough understanding and segmentation of your customer and prospect base, categorized by their potential.

Segment Coverage				
Segment	Number of Calls	Frequency of Calling	Annual Calls	Number of accounts with this Call Frequency & Totals
A	400	2x a Month	24	17
B	300	1x a Month	12	25
C	200	1x a Quarter	4	50
D	100	1x a Year	1	100
Totals	1,000			192

Account Coverage				
Customer Segment	Percent of Total Revenue	Number of Units Owned	Number of Accounts	Percent of Accounts
A	40%	Over 26	23	2%
B	30%	11 to 25	92	8%
C	20%	4 to 10	230	20%
D	10%	1 to 3	805	70%
Totals	100%		1,150	100%

Assessing the total potential of a customer account can be approached in various ways, with a straightforward method being the tally of major machinery units they possess. This count serves as a basis for classification, where customers with the highest number of units are designated as “A Accounts”, and those with the fewest as “D Accounts”, with "B" and “C Accounts” falling in intermediate categories.

The number of units is a strong indicator of an account's financial engagement, reflecting both their propensity to invest in new machinery and their expenditure on parts and maintenance. Over time, this metric reliably predicts the overall business potential of these accounts.

Ranking all accounts from highest to lowest based on machinery ownership often reveals a limited number of “A Accounts” and a substantial array of “D Accounts”. Our extensive experience working with dealer clientele indicates that approximately 2% fall into the "A" category, 8% into "B", 20% into "C", leaving a majority of 70% in the "D" category.

The essence of this segmentation lies in its revenue implications: "A Accounts" are projected to constitute 40% of potential revenue, with "B Accounts" contributing another 30%. Collectively, they represent 70% of your revenue, positioning the average account, in terms of potential revenue, within the "B" category.

Segmenting Prospects

It may be a common occurrence for your sales team to perceive the majority of accounts as falling within the "D" category, a perspective rooted in the average quantity of accounts and the machinery units they possess. While numerically predominant, these "D Accounts" do not generate sufficient business to be considered representative of an "average revenue account."

The pivotal question then becomes: where should your team's efforts be concentrated, and which accounts warrant comprehensive attention from your dealership? Clearly, given that "A" and "B Accounts" are responsible for generating 70% of your business, it's imperative that your strategies focus on acquiring and retaining these high-value clients.

Managing Revenue Producers

In our approach, we've categorized accounts by their total potential, a process known as "segmentation." The market share your dealership commands is intrinsically linked to how effectively you manage your "A" and "B Accounts". Faced with a market dynamic of fewer large accounts and a multitude of smaller ones, the critical decision revolves around whether to target the smaller, high-volume segment at the top of the market or the larger, low-volume segment at the bottom.

Referring back to our earlier discussion on "coverage," it's our belief that your dealership's marketing efforts should be strategically allocated: 40% towards "A Accounts", which account for 40% of business, and 30% towards "B Accounts", with the remaining efforts distributed accordingly.

Focusing on an individual salesperson's contribution, let's consider a scenario where they are capable of making 5 calls per day, 4 days a week, throughout 50 weeks of the year, totaling 1,000 calls annually. This number represents the salesperson's "time inventory."

The question then becomes how best to allocate these 1,000 annual calls to maximize returns. Should 40% be dedicated to "A Accounts" and 30% to "B Accounts"? Given the paramount importance of "A Accounts", it's advisable for salespeople to engage with them most frequently. The table provided [above/below] offers a guide on prioritizing a salesperson's annual calls based on account significance, detailing the call frequency per account type and the consequent number of accounts a salesperson can feasibly manage. In this model, a salesperson can effectively cover approximately 200 accounts.

Analyze & Organize

This scenario may not precisely mirror your dealership's current circumstances, yet it serves as an illustrative guide on structuring the call activities of sales personnel and realistically estimating the number of accounts they can manage.

Consider a proficient salesperson who can execute 1,000 calls annually and is capable of extending their reach to, for instance, 250 accounts. This prompts reflection on the actual coverage extent and the number of accounts that remain unattended. Contrary to the initial 634 accounts initially proposed, a more feasible and effective number should be considered.

The strategic organization of sales endeavors within a dealership falls under the purview of sales managers and business owners. As a dealership manager, your responsibilities extend beyond mere financial or asset management; they encompass the optimal allocation of your team's most precious commodity – their time.

We advocate for a thorough review of your sales coverage and the adoption of a structured account management methodology, which involves:

- Organizes prospective and active accounts by size.
- Allocates sale's time based on annual number of calls and frequency of calls by account size.
- Assigns accounts by salesperson and determines how to cover those accounts that fall into the "C" and "D" categories.

Assigning Accounts to Salespeople

So what do you do with all these accounts grouped by size and priority, and now some definition of how many calls salespeople can accomplish? Well the obvious next step is to start organizing the accounts into groups that can be "covered" by the salespeople. If you found that your market has 3% of the accounts doing 40% of the business and that is 45 accounts, you have some decisions to make. Do you give all the "A Accounts" to one or two salespeople (major account salespeople)? Or do you spread this around the number of salespeople?

Now you're beginning to see what your job really is about. You job is to start making these hard decisions. You need to start deciding how many accounts by size, priority, location and many other factors you want assigned to each salesperson. Think about the chart below:

		Split 1		Split 2	
Segment	# of Accts	Customers	Prospects	Customers	Prospects
A	6	2	4	4	2
B	10	4	6	8	2
C	24	8	16	18	6
D	160	40	120	120	40
Total	200	54	146	150	50
		27.0%	73.0%	75.0%	25.0%

The sales manager in "Split 1" decided this salesperson needs to focus on breaking into new accounts and finding more business. The "Split 2" is a different approach, here the sales manager has told the salesperson "keep the existing accounts and penetrate their spending so that they spend more of their money with our company."

Just picking the number of accounts for a salesperson is not all that there is to this process. You need to look at your sales grand strategy, your sales tactics, your manufacturer's current focus and available products, then you need to look at the salespeople's skills, experience and your compensation plan. You still need to look at things such as the geographic location of some accounts. While we talk about "assigning accounts" to salespeople, it does not mean that we are ignoring the windshield time that salespeople would experience if their accounts are all over the country.

So in this step you pick the strategy you want to focus on, the tactics you want your salespeople to use, the number of accounts they can handle, the focus of "dig for new business" or "cultivate the existing business." Then you have to look at geography, experience and many other factors, this is getting to the senior management decision making responsibility you were hired for. Your job is to get results out of the sales force.

Some sales managers have gone to their salespeople and said, here is how many calls I believe you can handle. I want you to call these large accounts this often, the medium ones like this, and the small one once a year, therefore you can handle "X" number of accounts in each size, pick what you want, but not over the limit of "X." And then anything not "assigned" to salespeople has to be covered by new salespeople not in existence at the company.

The final point here is that this is not impossible to do, it just requires someone making some real decisions and then watching the results and making adjustments into the future as things progress.

Developing Your Target Customer Philosophy

Many choices are possible, what you do with them is part of your company's package of value and what will make you unique. Do you want to address selling "competitively priced products," "quality merchandise," or "cost of ownership" to name a few. From these grand strategy decisions you will then see that companies will be more receptive or less receptive to your style and that will influence who you target.

Selecting Target Accounts

Certainly, your existing customers are your first and best audience. If the grand strategy we were just talking about is radically different than what you have been offering your customers you will want to determine what the impact would be in customer retention and deeper penetration.

Usually target accounts are selected by a company because they fit in categories of profile you have created for your sales strategy. These accounts might own a competitor's brand which you believe you can replace; they might have a purchasing philosophy or be of a certain size that you believe you service well.

Closing Reluctant Customers

While we can't control the customer's speed, we can control our approach. Focus on building trust, understanding their needs, and showcasing why they should act now, not later. We are dependent on their speed . Highlight the cost of inaction.

Show them what happens if they stay stuck in the status quo. This isn't about pushing your solution; it's about helping them see the fire under their seat. Their costs or pain can come in many ways. It might be increased maintenance costs, personal or employee safety, productivity, or the price increase from your manufacturer that is coming.

Second, customers aren't mind readers (shocking, right?). They stumble, stall, and wander throughout the buying journey. By becoming their change management sherpa, guiding them through the process, we can slash the sales cycle like a pro.

Using the magic of objective-based selling, we've seen win rates skyrocket and sales cycles shrink by 30-40%. That's the power of understanding their journey and helping them navigate it with confidence.

You can conceive of the total market as a box, and your customers are all clustered in one corner. Then there are your target prospects, general prospects, and suspects; together, these groups comprise the entire market. Where should you work first? On your existing accounts, then on the target prospects because you probably know more about them and understand their potential business for your company.

Conducting Competitive Analysis

Competition Worksheet

Company	Ownership	Brands	Equipment Sales Performance	Aftermarket Sales Performance	Financial Performance	Customer Satisfaction	Visibility
Competition A							
Competition B							
Competition C							
Competition D							
Your Company							
Attach Geographic Maps of Each Company's Area of Responsibility by Brand. Attach Individual Sheets of SWOT (Strength, Weakness, Opportunities & Threats							

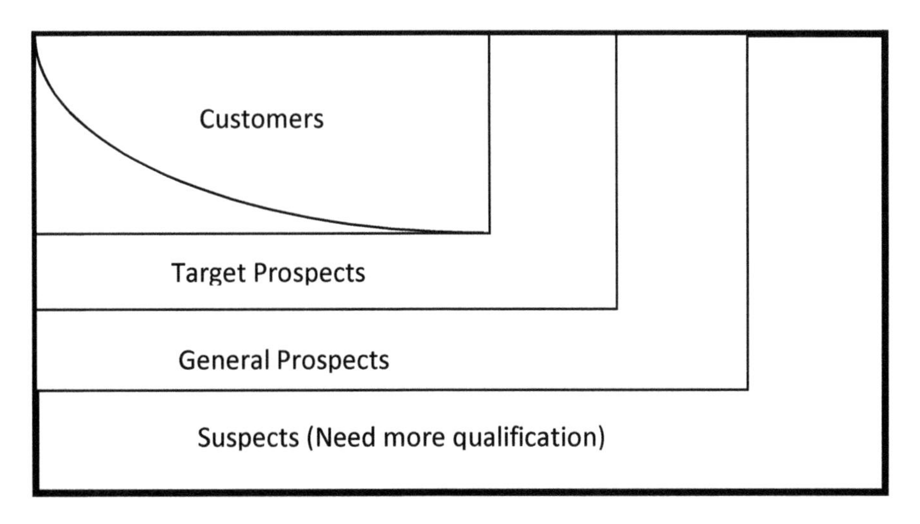

The sales manager who says we are so go that we have no competition is either blind or stupid. Maybe both! If you are good, someone is trying to take your business away from your customers. So, who are they? Where are they? How many salespeople do they have?

What products do they sell, and what are the comparison points between theirs and yours? These are some of the points you should be asking and looking at analyzing.

You might look at organizing your review and comparison of your competitors in a similar chart.

This chart is only an illustration of some of what you might want to consider and review about your competition. Don't forget to objectively assess your company to see how you compare to the competition. Using a chart like this, you may identify the strengths and weaknesses of your company and your competitors.

Compensation

There are various ways to approach designing compensation for employees. Traditionally, we have paid salaries, hourly wages, or commissions. Each of these has its own features and liabilities.

- Salary is designed to compensate someone for their full attention and effort in our business. Salary is generally used with career-oriented people, some who are college graduates, but the expectation is that they are very personally motivated.
- Hourly wages are frequently used for production employees who are considered interchangeable. They are paid to execute designs from others. Seldom are they expected to be creative or be responsible for expanding the scope of the business.
- Commission has traditionally been reserved for sales activities. Like "piece work pay," we reward the salesperson for accomplishment and seldom for the actual tasks leading up to the sale.

The most critical aspect of compensation is how it supports the company's mission and strategies.

Each of these compensation styles has its benefits and its limitations. Over the years, people have blended portions of them together, even augmented them with monetary bonuses or perks, like trips, cars, or car allowances. The most critical aspect of compensation is how it supports the company's mission and strategies.

Designing a compensation plan to integrate with a strategy is more complex than choosing between salary or commission.

A quick illustration of this strategic compensation will make the point. A manufacturer recognized their company's considerable potential in obtaining and controlling the service business on the capital goods products they sold. Extensive work went into identifying various service products that they provided units 15%, parts 7%, and labor 5%. About one year later, someone in the "sales" department changed the basic compensation design to a straightforward plan. The new plan eliminated any earnings or reward to the salespeople for selling scheduled maintenance, extended warranty, or extensive rebuild to existing products. This new plan focuses on selling new units. In fact, it is a simple straight percentage of gross profit on those new units.

Consider this from the salespersons' standpoint. While taking care of all the needs of a customer will help get them in the door or keep them there. They will only get paid for selling new units. Good and seasoned salespeople will still sell service, parts, and even rentals because it is good for the customer. Newer and inexperienced salespeople with little relationship skills will focus on the task of selling new units. Now don't get me wrong, there's nothing wrong with selling new units. The point to understand from this story is that the change in compensation was a change in strategies. If the issues were that the production line was standing idle, the market share was slipping, and the backlog of techs getting to the customer was lengthening, then the change may have been appropriate.

With this illustration as a backdrop, let's discuss some possibilities.

Sales compensation is the most frequent target when discussing design in this area. Owners are seeking ways to motivate salespeople to move iron.

- Dealership A is looking to garner more of the total spending done by its customers in their line of business. They have analyzed the existing and historic sales patterns. They found that they get about 25% of the market total sales in their area, and customers do their own service 38% of the time. Competitors seem to work on 15% of their equipment.

The principal of this company wanted to increase the number of units sold that included either extended warranty or full maintenance contracts. He decided to:

- Establish a base salary for salespeople of $20,000.
- Pay 10% of gross profit on every unit sold without a service agreement.
- Pay 25% of gross profit for every unit sold with an approved service agreement.

Can you see the strategy in this design?

1) Dealership B is concerned about increasing both market share and gross profit. In looking at the critical variables and national averages in their industry, they want to double their market share while doubling their gross profit percentage. Their compensation looks like this:

- The $30,000 base is paid in 12 monthly installments.
- An incentive of $50,000 will be paid in four quarterly installments if the salesperson achieves a particular market share for the counties they cover. Failure to reach the target means NO INCENTIVE is paid.
- Also, an incentive pool of $40,000 is available in four quarterly installments if the salesperson reaches 12% gross profit on the invoiced units that quarter.

Company B is strategically creating a performance target. While some companies pay a particular portion of the gross profit on every sale, this company needs to create such a gap for the salesperson attaining success that the total result of the effort moves them across the finish line.

This would be similar to two football teams; one pays their players for every goal scored the other pays for every game won. While scoring goals is undoubtedly part of winning the game, it ignores the possibility that the other team could score more goals. Our team could score more goals and earn more money than last year, yet lose every game. The second design greatly enhances our chance of winning the game and probably the championship.

2) Considering Company C, they are doing well in market share. Their service organization is performing at record levels, but gross profit has decreased on unit sales. They chose a different plan.

GP%	Commission %
10%	20%
12%	24%
14%	28%
16%	32%
18%	36%

- $25,000 draw against commission.
- They are using a stepped commission plan of:

It's not complex, but it meets the company's strategic needs.

3) There can be many variations based on a company's strategic needs. Company D had identified a large group of products they wanted to be represented by their salespeople. They structured the compensation plan as follows:

- $250 for every unit sold.
- $50 for every P.M. agreement.
- $80 for each month's rent
- $100 for every product rebuild.

While the numbers may differ in your industry, they represent a different approach to paying salespeople. They are not right or wrong, merely different.

4) Our final example is one of the salespeople in the aftermarket department. Here the manager was looking to increase the penetration of the accounts and add new accounts. He wanted to encourage the salespeople to work with the larger accounts because they had the most units in the area. This strategy for increasing the customer share and developing new accounts came out in a compensation plan as:

A. Based on the top fifty accounts from last year, the salesperson is paid 3% of sales.
B. Any new account brought in by the salesperson would receive 5% of sales from those accounts for 12 months.

This program is heavy in its strategic design. The manager believed that the top fifty existing accounts probably were a significant amount of last year's business. Sometimes these top accounts can represent 40-50% of the sales volume.

The manager wanted these accounts to be significant to the salesperson. The larger they could grow the accounts, the more of the company's total business from the accounts.

Next, the commission on the top fifty accounts was not planned to be enough for a salesperson to live comfortably. The push had to be to get new accounts.

For this company, their major suppliers set quotas for their parts purchasing. Before the new commission change, the company reached only 50% of those parts quotas. After the program was in place for a few months, they averaged 94% of those quotas.

Indeed, other activities and good management were needed to reach the results in this last example, but the compensation design complemented management's efforts. We've illustrated some ways to implement your strategy through a compensation program.

There are other considerations you may need to include in your plans. For some employees, you will want to consider the balance between fixed and variable pay. While some employees are very concerned about the consistency of their pay, there exists a certain level they are willing or capable of risking. This level will be different for each employee.

	Fixed	**Variable**
Secure	Salary	
At Risk	Bonus	Comm

When GM was negotiating with the UAW at Saturn, part of the pay plan was for the employees to achieve goals. The goals were heavily influenced by teamwork. Additionally, GM had asked the workers to take base hourly pay equal to 80% of the national UAW contract. The bargaining unit didn't want the amount of pay at risk through performance evaluation to exceed X %. This exemplifies how performance can be blended into the compensation plan.

Recently in designing a pay plan for a branch manager, we looked at establishing a base complemented by a bonus pool. We then modified the pool based on the manager's performance within a set of agreed-upon goals. Use the numbers below to illustrate this performance design.

Base Pay$30,000

<u>Available Bonus$40,000</u>

Potential Earnings$70,000

Illustration Goals

Market Share	XX%
Net Profit	XX%
CSI	XX%

For illustration, let's say the three goals are equal in importance. Our method of evaluating success could simply be the percentage of the goal attained. So, if the manager reached the market share number, that would be 100% of the goal. Reaching 90% of the net profit target and 100% of the CSI goal would yield results as seen in the table below:

Illustration Goals

	Goal	**% Attained**	**Weighting Factor**	**Extended Weighting**
Market Share	XX%	100%	33%	33%
Net Profit	XX%	90%	33%	30%
CSI	XX%	100%	33%	33%
				96%

From the above information, we would then modify the available bonus only to pay out 96% of the total; therefore, the manager would make the:

Base	30,000 x	100% =	30,000
Bonus	40,000 x	96% =	
Total Paid			

How you finally design your compensation plan is not as important as knowing it will support your strategy. Be patient with yourself. This is not a science; it is an art. Getting results lies not in the compensation plan but in the manager. The compensation plan is a support to good managers. Poor managers will blame the results on the compensation plan, the competition, the economic conditions, or their lack of quality support.

Good management understands how to use a compensation plan. They blend it into reward systems, they use it to recognize employees who succeed, and they understand that it can be a portion of the scorecard. Well-designed compensation plans are fair, encourage employees to reach goals, and are not static. As the organization grows, the products change and the business evolves from one phase to another, the compensation programs will need to change.

Compensation Designs

A properly designed salesperson's compensation system can help attract and retain top salespeople and direct their daily activities.

But compensation alone will not provide for high salesperson morale and motivation. As you design your compensation program, you must also take into consideration factors in addition to compensation which affect sales results.

Purposes Of A Salesperson Compensation Program

The purposes of a salesperson compensation program are to

- attract quality salespeople.
- retain quality salespeople.
- direct salespeople activities.

Attract Quality Salespeople

To attract the kinds of talent you want, your compensation program must be lucrative enough to make you competitive. This does not mean that you have to be the "high bidder" in the market, but you do need to be in the right general range. Your own skills as a salesperson will help you convince your preferred recruit to come work for you.

In some time periods, you may be able to offer less, while in other time periods you may have to offer more. The competition in the "talent market" will determine what you have to offer.

Top talent requires a greater investment than mediocre talent. It is important for you to determine exactly what you want in the way of sales talent before you begin to compete for that talent in the market.

Retain Quality Salespeople

The "talent market" will also determine, to a large extent, how much you have to pay to retain salespeople. Your competitors for talent will be willing to pay more for your top salespeople than they will be willing to pay for your mediocre performers.

The incentive portion of your compensation program is designed to motivate salespeople to do what you want them to do. Therefore, those who do best get paid the most. That means they are much more expensive in the talent market, discouraging talent competitors from "buying" them.

Help Managers Direct Salespeople Activities

Managing a group of salespeople is different from managing most other types of workers. That is because selling is a different type of job, with different tasks and challenges.

- Selling is a solo profession. Generally, salespeople travel alone during their work. As a result, they tend to develop their own styles of selling, adopting some good habits and some bad habits. Because a sales manager cannot observe and direct the daily activities of a salesperson, he or she needs the support of a compensation system that encourages them to do what the company wants them to do.

- Selling is lonely and often discouraging. Even the best salespeople don't expect to sell everything to everybody all the time. Because of the rejection they face in their selling activities, salespeople need a supportive environment within their companies. A compensation system can help provide the positive feedback a good salesperson needs regularly.
- Salespeople see more of their customers than they do of their boss or company. As a result, they may become highly sympathetic to their customers-so sympathetic that they may be working more for their customers than for the company. Successful salespeople are empathetic to their customers, but always remember their job is to sell what the company has at the highest possible prices. A well-designed compensation system can help reinforce this challenge.
- Salespeople feel a need to be liked by their customers. Because of this need, they are naturally hesitant to be "tough" when toughness is needed-such as in a negotiation on pricing or adjustments. A well-designed compensation system can help.
- Salespeople are logistically more difficult to supervise. As a result, managing requires certain types of tools that may not be as important for other jobs. One of the best tools for helping you manage your salesforce is a well-designed compensation system.
- Salespeople look for messages in little things. Good salespeople are highly sensitive to "messages" they receive. A well-designed compensation system sends financial messages to salespeople about what to do and where to spend their time.

A compensation program is the best means of communicating the company's goals and marketing strategies to its salesforce. As such, a good salesperson's compensation program can be a powerful tool for helping your business reach its goals.

Morale And Motivation

A well-designed compensation plan for salespeople can help your dealership reach its goals. Nevertheless, the compensation program alone will not provide you with the success you desire.

Salespeople are your most important talent resource. As with other resources that you utilize, they require maintenance and care.

Anything affecting their morale and motivation can (and probably will) result in an increase or decrease in sales.

Salespeople are vulnerable to dejection and loss of confidence. There is an inherent loneliness in many selling situations. Further, salespeople are subjected to the self-doubt that follows the loss of an account.

A sales force with low morale will provide sub-standard performance. Therefore, maintaining good morale is as important as any job you do as sales manager.

Morale and motivation are closely linked and are based on an individual's needs and values. Each salesperson may be motivated by different needs. As one need is fulfilled, a salesperson will be motivated by the next need in the list. The different types of needs include the following:

- A feeling of security
- A feeling of belonging
- A feeling of being appreciated
- A feeling of growing

A Feeling Of Security

Salespeople need a sense of job security and a predictable income. Salespeople also need to understand what is expected of them and what will happen to them if those expectations are not met. They will feel secure when they perform up to clearly understood expectations and are treated fairly.

A Feeling Of Belonging

Salespeople also need to have a sense of belonging. They need to feel that they are part of some larger organization or group of people who share common goals and concerns and who work together to achieve things that they cannot achieve alone.

Salespeople desire to feel that they are part of a team effort and they will be motivated by team goals. Salespeople should have feelings of pride about their contributions to the company.

A Feeling Of Being Appreciated

Salespeople feel appreciated when they feel they are making a contribution to the goals of the organization and that other people in the organization acknowledge their contribution. Salespeople desire praise and recognition. They will feel appreciated when they do something well and their efforts are acknowledged.

A Feeling Of Growing

Salespeople should have a sense of growth-the feeling that they are becoming more knowledgeable and more skilled every year. They should have an ever-increasing baseline of knowledge to prove it. Salespeople thrive on new challenges. Each salesperson will be motivated to some extent by each of the preceding needs. Your salespeople will perform most effectively when all these needs are met.

A well-designed compensation system is only a part of an effective management program. When the other factors such as clearly defined goals, clear expectations, a feeling of belonging and appreciation, and the opportunity for salespeople to grow are present, a compensation system can play a vital role in helping a company meet its goals.

Comfort Zones

People have a tendency to take the path of least resistance. Since most salespeople have sales volume opportunities beyond what they can reasonably accomplish, they will naturally spend their time on the easiest tasks. In the absence of an incentive system to reward them for doing more difficult tasks, they will usually do the tasks they are comfortable doing.

"Comfortable tasks" might include:

- Calling on current customers exclusively
- Selling solely those products with which they are familiar
- Selling the easiest-to-sell items
- Cutting price instead of justifying value

The inevitable result of salespeople calling only on current customers is a decline in business volume. Salespeople who make only the comfortable calls on current customers are sure to see their sales drop over time.

When salespeople sell only those products with which they are. familiar, introducing new products becomes extremely difficult. In the history of almost every product, it is most profitable when it is new, before everybody else has something similar. A salesforce that sells only familiar, older products cannot capitalize on the higher profitability available with new products.

When salespeople sell only the "easiest-to-sell items;' they are probably costing their company profitability. A product that is easy to sell will not generally carry the profit margin of a product that is more difficult to sell.

When salespeople take the path of least resistance and cut the price instead of justifying value, they are giving away money. When a salesperson cuts the price, he/she not only costs your dealership profitability, he/she also sets a precedent that makes it more difficult to get the correct (higher) price in the future.

In selling, there are tasks that are comfortable and pleasant, and there are tasks that are uncomfortable and unpleasant. Your greatest return on your investment in salespeople comes when they do the uncomfortable tasks.

Uncomfortable tasks may include:

- Making "cold calls" on prospects
- Taking accounts away from competitors
- Negotiating higher prices
- Selling new products
- Selling more difficult-to-sell, higher-margin products
- Value-added work such as fleet surveys and scrap tire analysis

If your salespeople are not doing uncomfortable tasks, it may not be because of a flaw in your compensation program. It is possible they lack confidence in your company or its products. Before you are too critical of your salespeople, take a look at how well other areas of your company are functioning. You should not blame your salespeople for problems they cannot control. In the absence of an incentive program, salespeople will not generally do uncomfortable tasks. Yet, your greatest return is when they do those uncomfortable tasks that will help your sales volume and profitability grow.

You need to encourage and motivate your salespeople to do the uncomfortable tasks-to move outside their comfort zones.

The incentive component of a compensation system is designed to encourage salespeople to move outside their comfort zones. It provides a financial reward for doing difficult tasks those difficult tasks that provide to your dealership the greatest return on money invested in sales talent.

Basics Of A Good Compensation Program

There are four factors to consider in designing a compensation program for salespeople:

- Safety
- Incentive
- Control
- Cost

Safety

"Safety" is the degree of risk that a salesperson takes in comparison to his/her minimum living requirements. If there is little risk that his/her minimum living requirements will be met, then the plan is "safe." If there is substantial risk, then the program is unsafe, or "high risk." In order for salespeople to work successfully, they must believe that the compensation program will meet their minimum living requirements.

In any compensation program, the amount not guaranteed is the amount at risk. The portion at risk is the incentive portion, because the amount at risk is also the opportunity for the salesperson to maximize his/her earnings.

As you design your own program, it will be useful for you to think in terms of "safety and incentive" as opposed to "salary and commission." The safe portion of the compensation program should probably be salary, and the at-risk part should be the incentive (or commission) portion.

Incentive

Good salespeople are goal setters. A well-designed compensation system should tell them how to establish goals. When a salesperson looks at a compensation plan, it should say to him/her, "These are the rules within which you can maximize your earnings."

The incentive portion of a compensation program is designed to create motivation. Incentives may be emotional or financial. The recognition program should focus on the emotional aspects of motivation, while the compensation program should focus on the financial aspects of motivation.

In order to be effective, incentive pay must always be at-risk. It must be clearly understood that this portion of pay will only be earned when predetermined performance levels are met. Therefore, a commission program which virtually ensures a salesperson that his/her minimum living requirements will be met will provide little or no incentive in the "safe" portion (that portion ensured of being met).

Incentive compensation is intended to provide motivation, but when it is designed incorrectly, it can lead to de-motivation. There are two factors to consider:

- **Attainability.** If salespeople feel that high possible earnings are realistically unattainable, they will tend to view the program as an exercise in trickery; this will de-motivate them.
- **Fairness.** Salespeople must view the program as "fair" when compared to competition and other employers in the area, and fair as it applies to each of the salespeople in your dealership. "Fair" is highly subjective, and salespeople may view something as unfair which you perceive as completely fair.

Incentive pay should be based on individual goals for salespeople which, when achieved, support the dealership goals. Payment for achievement of the goals should be large enough to be meaningful. Further, the payment should be soon enough after goal achievement that the achievement/reward relationship is obvious.

Control

The compensation program must always direct your salespeople toward the accomplishment of company goals. Since salespeople work alone for the most part, the compensation system should send messages to them about what it is you want them to do.

In general, a "safe" (largely salary) program allows you more direct control, since salespeople see their salary dependent on doing what their supervisor tells them to do. An at-risk (largely commission) program depends on compensation messages to exert the same level of influence.

A safe program requires much greater day-to-day effort on the part of the sales manager. Without an at-risk incentive portion of the compensation program, the sales manager must provide more hands-on direction. The program must exert control and, at the same time, be flexible enough to change due to market conditions, sales territories, individual salesperson's needs, etc.

You will want to design a system that uses currently available information, or information that can be obtained relatively easily with your system. Nevertheless, don't allow your accounting system to determine your compensation program. If you need additional data (and that additional data will require new or different reports), investing the time, money and energy into obtaining those reports may be a good investment.

Cost

Salespeople represent your most important investment. Since they are the people (the resources) who acquire business for your dealership, they will not come cheaply if you want valuable talent.

Some compensation plans cost more than others. It is important that you calculate the costs of various compensation plan alternatives and their expected return on investment prior to implementation.

One of your primary considerations will be the amount of fixed costs (or overhead) versus variable costs in your compensation program. Many companies are attempting to reduce fixed costs and make as many costs as possible variable.

Other Factors

As you have read, the four basic factors of a good compensation program are safety, incentive, control and cost.

Before you design your own program, there are two additional factors to consider:
Contribution and Simplicity

Contribution

A compensation program is always best when the salesperson's compensation can be directly related to his/her contribution to the company's goals. This is seen as ultimately fair and provides a common understanding of performance.

The compensation program is easiest to design when gross profit is the only measure of contribution. When other factors such as customer service, landing new accounts, training new salespeople, selling more difficult-to-sell or more profitable items or working with other salespeople on shared accounts are important, contribution is more difficult to measure.

> Your compensation plan MUST support the goals of your company!
>
> To be effective, a compensation plan must be easy for salespeople to understand and easy for you to administer.

For contribution to be measured effectively, goals for each salesperson must be established in advance. These goals must be measurable within the accounting system of your dealership and understood by the salesperson.

One of the most common problems of many compensation systems is that they send messages inconsistent with the overall goals of the company. For example, a company may want to build its business by landing new accounts. This may mean that sales and/or profitability suffer for the short-term as salespeople spend large amounts of time with new prospects. While that may be acceptable to management in its overall strategic plan, if the compensation plan is based entirely on volume, the chance of the dealership achieving its goals is reduced and the salespeople experience reduced income.

Simplicity

To be effective, a compensation plan must be easy for salespeople to understand and easy for you to administer.

Different Salespeople, Different Plans

Not all salespeople in your business have to be on the same compensation plan.

There may be many reasons for you to have one type of plan for one salesperson and a different plan for another.

For example:

- When a salesperson is new with you, you may elect to put him/her on straight salary for a time, and then gradually change him/her to a different plan.
- If you hire retirees who might do an excellent job for you in certain tasks or with certain customers, but who don't want their earnings to exceed a certain level.
- When you need to address particular problems with a salesperson or encourage him/her to change his/her habits.

While it is important that your salespeople feel your plan is fair, that doesn't mean that all your salespeople must be on the same plan.

What Do You Want To Achieve?

In designing your compensation system, think in terms of a scale with "safety" on one end of the scale and "incentive" on the other end of the scale.

Regardless of what you choose to call a compensation plan, these two items are opposite each other. The more safety for salespeople you build into your plan, the less financial incentive there is for them to produce the results you want. The more financial incentive you build into your plan, the less safety for your salespeople.

You can design your program to help achieve your company's goals. Consider the following examples:

More Management Control Of Salespeople Activities

There are two ways to control and direct salespeople: either by continual daily supervision or by sending messages through the compensation system.

If a program is on the safe end of the scale, you can better control and direct your salespeople through daily supervision. Since salespeople are paid independent of performance, they will respond more readily to supervisors' requests. For example, a salesperson paid on the safe end of the scale will probably not resent having to take his/her selling time to train a new salesperson. On the other hand; a salesperson paid on the incentive end of the scale might see training as a costly use of his/her selling time.

A program on the safe end of the scale requires more daily supervision since there are few messages in the compensation system about how a salesperson should spend his/her time. If you wish to control and direct your salespeople by means of the compensation system, you would want to design your program to be heavily loaded toward the incentive end of the scale.

Programs which are heavily incentive-based tend to attract salespeople who are entrepreneurial risk takers. They do what the compensation program "tells" them to do. As a result, the program must be very carefully designed so it sends the messages you want it to send.

Higher Sales Volume/Gross Profit

If your goal is to increase sales volume or gross profit, your program should be structured toward the incentive end of the scale.

Incentive generates motivation; since salespeople paid on the incentive end of the scale are paid only based on the gross profit of what they sell, they will be highly focused on sales volume and gross profit.

Safe-paid salespeople may become complacent since there is no financial incentive to excel and no penalty for not excelling. Some salespeople may take the attitude "I get paid whether they buy or not" and, consequently, not exert maximum effort.

Better Customer Relations

If improved customer relations is your goal, you may want to consider the safe end of the scale. Since making the next sale is not foremost in the salesperson's mind, a safe-paid salesperson may spend extra time listening to customers and uncovering their true needs and problems. He/she may be more inclined to provide value-added services than an incentive-paid salesperson. Incentive-paid salespeople might consider value-added services, such as fleet surveys, a waste of valuable selling time. Further, safe-paid salespeople tend to be less "pushy" and more concerned about long-term customer relations.

Lower Costs

A safe-pay plan (such as straight salary) provides lower costs per dollar of sales as sales volume increases. Since compensation is fixed, the amount paid to salespeople as sales rise is continually less per dollar of sales.

An incentive-pay plan (such as straight commission) provides lower overall costs as sales volume decreases. Since compensation is variable, the amount paid to salespeople is less if volume is lower.

If you believe sales will increase, you can make more money per unit and make more total profit by paying salary to your salespeople. But you will have better luck getting that sales increase if you pay on commission.

Fixed Versus Variable Costs

If you want to reduce fixed costs, you should consider incentive-pay plans. With these plans, the cost of selling varies with sales volume and gross profit. Safe-pay plans have fixed costs that do not vary with sales volume and gross profit.

There are advantages and ·disadvantages to each type of pay plan. You must determine what your goals are and. structure your plan accordingly.

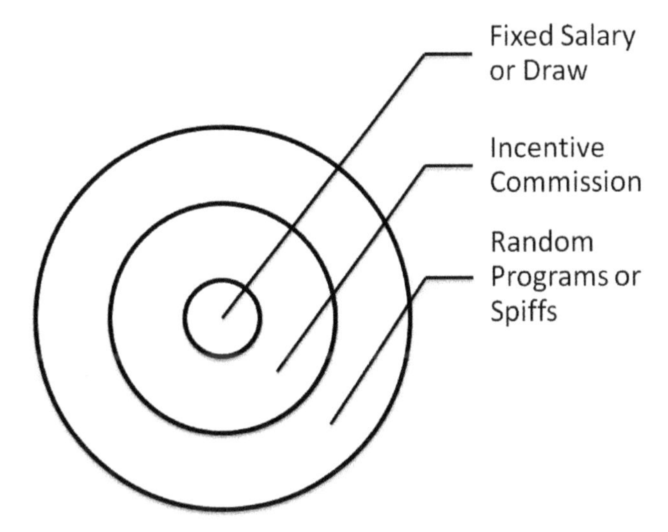

Designing Your Plan

Establishing The Safe Portion

In establishing the safe portion of the compensation plan, your primary interests should include:

- competition in the talent market.
- minimum living requirements.

The safe portion of your earnings plan will largely be determined by the amount of money you are forced to spend to attract and retain quality salespeople. This is determined by the market for talent (what competing firms are willing to pay for the same talent).

Make sure as you calculate the safe portion that you take into consideration your entire package, including compensation, benefits and additional opportunities. Things such as training, company vehicle, promotion opportunities, profit sharing, health benefits and ownership opportunity are important to consider as a part of your overall package.

The second consideration is what salespeople believe they must be assured of making to meet their minimum living requirements. When salespeople are not sure they will make their minimum living requirement, they are constantly on the lookout for a new job. Further, they tend to over-pressure prospects and customers to buy, damaging the goodwill which exists between you and your market.

If your compensation plan is a salary/commission plan, top salespeople will universally believe they will earn a portion of the incentive pay. They believe a portion of the commission is "safe." Therefore, you may be able to offer slightly less than their minimum living requirement and still attract the talent you want.

Establishing The Incentive Portion

To design the incentive portion of the plan, you must refer to the Dealership Financial Model.

Let's assume some of your compensation will be salary and some will be incentive (commission). To determine the amount available for incentive, subtract the salary portion from the total budget for sales compensation.

The result is the amount available to be distributed to salespeople in the form of commission.

Keep in mind that the purpose of the incentive portion is to

- provide motivation.
- send messages about what you want done.

Regardless of the payment method you select, you can determine the amount available for salespeople compensation using the above method. A well-designed compensation program supports and reinforces the company's goals, and the first of these goals is to meet the financial plan

Testing Your Plan

As you design and periodically redesign your compensation program, you need to remember that no compensation plan is perfect. It needs to be as consistent as possible, but flexible enough to meet the changing needs of the salespeople and the company.

Regardless of Your best efforts, no plan will ever be perfect. Your intention in testing the plan before it is presented to the salespeople is to locate the potential problem areas as soon as possible.

When testing the plan, first calculate each salesperson's earnings for the preceding two years as though they had been paid on the new plan. Then compare their earnings on the new plan with their earnings on your current plan. Ask yourself these questions:

- Are the earnings similar?
- Do the differences reflect what it is you want to achieve with the new plan?
- What motivational problems might the new plan create?
- How will each salesperson react?
- If you were a salesperson, what products and services would you sell?
- Is that in harmony with your objectives and the company goals?
- How could the plan be abused by the salespeople?

Make any changes necessary, then ask yourself the same questions again. After you have assured yourself of the validity of the new plan, take one or two of your top salespeople into your confidence. Tell them the purposes of the new plan, show them their earnings under the new plan as compared to the old plan and ask for their feedback. You may be surprised how differently they will see the new plan from how you see it.

Make necessary adjustments, then test and retest. A compensation plan is a powerful tool to help your dealership reach its goals. It deserves your best efforts.

Implementing The Plan

When you implement the plan, you can be sure you will receive one reaction from your salespeople: resistance. Even if the plan is better for them financially than the old plan, salespeople will resist the change.

Selling a new compensation system to salespeople is like selling any other product; you must stress the benefits of the new program.

To help salespeople adjust to the new plan, do two things: involve them in plan design before you finalize the plan, and hold a meeting with them at which you work through several compensation examples as a group.

Incentives & Random Programs

After working on all the variations of base, draw, salary and incentive sometimes it is good to remember that there are occasions in many sales groups when a special comes up, the manufacturer decides 6 months later to push a certain product, or you have some items (heavens it couldn't be old inventory!) that you want to have the salespeople focus on that you had not planned in your compensation design. This is when you have to have that extra money in your budget for a special promotion, spiff, or program that is not part of the "commission plan" and you would not want it to remain part of a plan; but you want to do something to motivate the salespeople for a week or four months. Did you remember to put that extra money in your "budget" or design at the beginning? This is a recommendation that you allocate some money for this function. As sure as it will rain in England, and snow in Minnesota, you'll come to a time when you want that extra money available.

If your plan called for 30% of gross profit for sales compensation, you might plan 15% for commission draw, 10% for commission above draw and 5% for random programs that you know will come and go.

The point here is to plan for this extra amount before you complete the entire commission design.

Expense Coverage

What sales department does not have expenses? There are some, but they generally come up as a different type of salesperson structure, like sales representatives. But in these cases the commission is frequently higher for them as they handle their own expenses. So if you have salespeople that are employees, what are your fixed or defined expenses beyond compensation, commission or payroll? Let's talk about some of the more familiar ones.

Cell phones

Many companies provide cell phones for salespeople now. In general, what we find when talking to our clients is that the company owns the cell phone, and in particular it means they own the phone number! This means that when a salesperson leaves the number stays with the company as well as the physical phone You might need to look at some options with this in your dealership.

When the cell phone or mobile number is included on the business card, literature or website the prospect or customer is calling the company and the company has information and details about those transactions. If the employee is providing their personal cell phone number (assuming the company provides phones) the company is losing connection information regarding the account and what might transpire in the future.

Setting limits on cell phone usage regarding personal use is generally determined by the company, the number of available minutes in the various plans and previous experience.

It could be helpful to have some of this outlined and documented in your company handbook, or in the salesperson's contract.

Computers

Does the company provide computer or does the salesperson? Sometimes this is as iterative a discussion as what comes first, the chicken or the egg? There are some protocols to consider if you are asking salespeople to handle company product information, account information, quotations and call history. If the salesperson owns the machine what access to the data do they have and how much? Who does the back up and where is it stored? If the salesperson leaves what is your access to their machine to eliminate and delete the data from your company and that of the manufacturers and accounts they have worked with.

Of course, you should be looking at the positive side also; these salespeople should be good salespeople with honor and integrity such that you trust them with this data whether it is your machine or theirs. Without this sort of information and data in today's world most salespeople cannot accomplish what they are being charged with.

Other points to think about though might be who pays for the software updates? Who makes sure that all computers are using the current version of programs? Are all computers using legal versions of all software; if not who is liable for the legal ramifications?

Medical Coverage

Medical coverage is different in various countries and companies. Each company has its own approach, but there are some areas to look at. Costs have changed over the years and in your company you probably have changed how you handle some of those costs.

How much, if any does the employee have to pay? Do you pay for single, dual and family coverage for all employees? Some companies pay for single, and the employee covers any variance from that level. Some companies pay for complete coverage no matter the situation. Generally the most important issue is to be consistent for all employees.

	Salesperson #1	Salesperson #2
Sales Revenue	$2,000,000	$1,000,000
Gross Profit Dollars	$240,000	$120,000
Gross Profit %	12%	12%
Compensation @30%	$72,000	$36,000
Medical Coverage Single Person for 1 Year	$12,000	$12,000
Commission & Medical Totals	$84,000	$48,000
Percent of Gross Profit Paid Out	**35%**	**40%**

But this is one of the larger expenses for many companies, and this is therefore one of the "fixed" costs that many sales managers need to consider in what the minimum and average performance levels for salespeople should be.

Look at this table and consider what the impact of medical coverage is based on different salespeople's performance levels.

Both salespeople are paid the same commission rate, have the same health care coverage and maintain the identical gross profit percentage. Yet one of them has a stronger impact on the percentage of gross profit dollars that the company has to spend, because they have a lower delivery of actual gross profit dollars.

While we don't' think this is a place to direct you on how much to pay of medical coverage, and certainly you need to be competitive in your local market to entice good performing salespeople to join your firm, you should keep some of this in mind when you set the benchmarks of performance for each level of salesperson and the compensation design.

Auto/Vehicle Coverage

Whether you pay a car or truck allowance for a salesperson or you provide the vehicle the amount of money you spend in this could be significant. Some companies treat this as a very strong fixed cost and just push the salespeople to keep their activity and volume up. Other companies have made this more variable.

One company we worked with looked at the amount of $500 a month for vehicle cost they were paying salespeople and wanted to see if they could make it more variable, in line with salespeople's performance. What they decided to do was to eliminate the "fixed $500 per month" and add additional commission if the salesperson sold a second used unit each month. Since they expected at least 2 or more used units to be sold, and the average used unit was $10,000; by increasing the commission rate on all 2nd units or more each month from 5% to 10% they made the opportunity to earn more than the $500 a significant possibility, and variablized the cost more for the company.

9. Customer Relationship Management - CRM

Implementing a CRM system tailored to the equipment industry

Each dealership is distinct, and it's probable that your industry has specific data that requires monitoring for each deal. In a CRM, you have the flexibility to tailor the stages of your sales and may find it necessary to incorporate custom fields to ensure you capture all the essential information required for successful deal closure.

Certainly, you'll require essential data points such as names, addresses, phone numbers, and email addresses for your customer base. A robust CRM system should delve into more nuanced details, including the number of units owned by each customer, the models, their age, condition, and replacement cycle. Based on your industry you might want to customize the CRM regarding the equipment to features of your equipment. Certainly the battery life in a golf car is considerably different than the battery life for a fork lift. And the lifting capacity is different in a fork lift than the voltage measurements in a generator. Look for a CRM that provides these sort of features. You also might discover needed features or fields down the road that you might want added. Make sure you have that flexibility without significant costs.

Customization and Flexibility

Consider having two to three contacts at each company. You want to have backups already in place if someone takes a promotion, transfer or leaves the company. After all the work you put into building a relationship with a prospect/customer you don't want to start from scratch all over again.

Effective organization of email communication is paramount. This involves grouping all email exchanges by the designated contact person within the customer's organization. This includes not only outgoing emails but also replies from the customer, all chronologically organized for easy reference. Make sure they are inside the CRM or directly accessible in the CRM. Also as sales manager you need to be able to see email correspondence between your salespeople and the customers. So this is not a "privacy" issue regarding communication, you need open transparency in emailsor quotes.

Backup and Security

Implementing robust security measures for customer and industry-sensitive data. You want good backups, and security to be sure you don't lose any data that you have invested time and money creating or collecting. You also want to review the access levels of salespeople. Should you allow every salesperson access to all accounts, and all information, or do salespeople only have access to their assigned accounts? Be sure to complying with any industry-specific privacy regulations

Integration is key for a seamless quoting process. Your CRM should seamlessly connect with both your quoting system and your manufacturer's system. This integration allows you to track created quotes, monitor their status (open or closed), investigate their outcomes, and attribute them to specific salespeople. There are benefits to salespeople of not doing double or triple entry when integrated. The most integrated ones require zero manual input as they allow voice transcription, identify callers, and assist in sending emails automatically. This streamlines salesman's ability to sell and not take as much time on paperwork. There is also the intangible benefit of the salesperson that hates doing paperwork, and their time is freed up from doing things that they don't like.

For comprehensive information dissemination to your sales team, your CRM should interface with your business system. This enables salespeople to access details about customer units being serviced, expected completion dates, and outstanding invoices.

Considering the input and update activities, a mobile-friendly CRM is indispensable. Salespeople should be able to access and update the CRM from their smartphones. I recommend a proactive approach — salespeople should open the CRM app before entering a client's business premises. Review recent history, quotes, and goals for this call. Salespeople might even dictate their goals into the CRM before the meeting. Post-call, while waiting for their vehicle's temperature to adjust, use the time to dictate a summary of the call and schedule the next one into their calendar.

BACKUP! BACKUP! BACKUP! And then consider where you keep the backups. Just as paper can burn, data in a computer can become the victim of corruption or theft. We generally recommend three to four levels or back up. Consider a few options here:

1. You have your data in your primary location. (On your server, in the cloud, etc.)
2. Where is your 1st level of backup? It should not be in the same location as your primary data.
3. You should have at least a daily back up, weekly, monthly, quarterly, and annual backups.
4. How much repair or re-entry of data in your CRM do you want to do if something happens to your data? How would you replace it?
5. If you are using a 3rd party CRM, do they back it up? How can you also back it up?

Implementation is crucial, and it starts at the top. If the sales manager doesn't actively use, monitor, and enforce compliance with the CRM, its effectiveness will diminish. Salespeople, often creatures of habit, may have their own methods. However, to achieve the goals outlined in this book, active engagement with the CRM is essential.

As a sales manager, regular discussions should revolve around adherence to scheduled calls, the quantity of calls made by each salesperson, the status of open quotes, and an exploration into why deals haven't been closed. Weekly reviews of reports on completed sales, open and closed quotes, upcoming calls, and missed calls are beneficial. As salespeople recognize that the CRM is the go-to source for information about their activities, behavioral changes will follow.

One of the recommendations we suggested earlier was having sales team meetings on a regular basis. Considering your "A" level accounts are only about 2-3% of your accounts this could be 15-50 accounts. Frequent team meetings could be yourself as sales manager, the assigned salesperson, the service manager, parts or rental manager, and for some accounts your dealer principal. Don't forget in these sales meetings to bring up the CRM account and review the calls, quotes, sales and forecast of what your team is expecting to happen with this account.

Expired Quote Management/Report is a significant help that one sales manager uses, it aids the sales team in not talking about the same 20 customers or quotes forever.

The CRM has helped that sales manager monitor that and make the team aware that they need to be using the CRM system.

Data Security and Privacy

As much as you want to put all of this information in the hands of your salespeople, you also need to consider if any data in your CRM is confidential, private or sensitive. If it is, that does not mean you don't share it, but you might limit some of the access, or the ability to do something with it. In fact, just sharing your data with salespeople is a balance between their need to know to accomplish their job with your need to limit their ability to take all of this data and go to the competition. Don't forget to include an NDA in your implementation of a CRM system.

You should consider how much data, or how wide a selection of data you wish to share with each salesperson. Some companies share only the assigned account information with a salesperson, other companies share all customer information in the CRM. Some CRM's have the ability to limit the data output, while allowing salespeople to add, update or access the data. Consider your companies policies and your management plans for this.

User Training and Onboarding

Training! Just as each new salesperson will need training on your CRM, if you are initiating a CRM with your sales force for the first time the entire team will need training. And don't think they will all get it the first time. You will need frequent training sessions. Then down the road, consider having some salespeople begin presenting how they use the CRM. You or your technical staff showed what you think it should do. But consider letting some of your better users show people what they "actually" do every day. Eventually, down the road ask certain salespeople to show some of the "hidden" features they use. You might have shown this initially, but many people might have skipped over that to just get started.

Working with your technical staff and human resources department develop a comprehensive training program for your sales team. Not only should you have a basic course, but you should have annual training. Maybe you have an annual sales team meeting before the new year. At that meeting include a 30-60 minute session on basic features and best practices. This is a tool that you need to continue reinforcing with your entire team.

Depending on your company size, you might need a dedicated CRM administrator. This person would continue to monitor the quality of the data. Correcting entries from salespeople that are not complete or have errors. They would be the person interfacing with the technical department on data storage, backups and software upgrades. If a salesperson added a new prospect, but the administrator finds that account already exists they would manage to merge of information. This is the person that would also work on the quality of your information. Have you thought about bringing information in from LinkedIn, Facebook, or industry association memberships to improve the quality of your information? Just having the names and addresses from your invoicing is not enough data for good customer relationship management. Some dealerships export the CRM address file and use services or utilities to compare and verify US Postal Address formatting for accurate mail delivery.

Your administrator should be the customer support person and CRM Maintenance expert. They should help in implementing a responsive customer support system. Your salespeople should see them as the front line of support and information. They are the person you rely on to handle regular maintenance to address bugs, updates, and system optimization.

Budgeting and ROI Analysis

Before we forget, you need to add an item to your annual budget for the CRM. What are the amortized costs of the initial purchase, the annual or monthly support charges, the wages and benefits for an administrator, and costs for other related data? In a number of industries, we work in, there is an organization who collects Financing Data (or UCC Filings) on any equipment which is purchased with financing. From that data they identify the equipment purchased, the company who purchased it, the financing company, and the brand of equipment. This is a great resource but is also an additional cost beyond your CRM fees. Because some industries do more financing than other UCC Filing information varies as to value based on the industry.

In addition to setting your budget, you should also consider how you are going to evaluate the ROI for your CRM. Conduct a periodic ROI analysis to assess the system's effectiveness.

Integration with Marketing Efforts

You want to be sure that your CRM is also capable of aligning with your market strategies.

When people come to your website you want to also match their user ID from the website information over to your CRM to capture new leads and current customer engagements.

Improving Marketing Efficiency

- Many leads created through marketing efforts go unnoticed.
- Often, leads not immediately prepared to purchase are overlooked rather than nurtured until they're ready.
- Numerous marketing teams lack clarity on the successes and failures of their strategies.
- There are various levels of complexity in marketing automation.
- This automation can assess the worth of leads by observing their actions.
- Marketing efforts can be synchronized with Customer Relationship Management (CRM) systems.
- Marketing also offers insights into how effective a campaign has been.
- Certain marketing tasks can be delegated to external services, available for a regular monthly payment.
- Choose systems that clearly demonstrate their return on investment to you.

Don't forget to pass new leads from the website onto salespeople. Then measure the length of time the salespeople take to follow up on those leads. A lead that appeared at your website this morning, might not still be interested tomorrow. Be sure to measure the conversion rate from leads to prospects. You also can track where your marketing efforts have the most impact by using a field in your CRM that checks for "How did you hear of us" or something like that. You might discover that emails have more effect for you than website, or TV at 11pm at night could have more impact than newspaper advertising.

Addressing Resistance to Change

Recognizing and addressing potential resistance from the sales team is a critical aspect of successful CRM implementation. Salespeople, often accustomed to their existing methods and routines, may initially perceive the adoption of a CRM system as disruptive or time-consuming. To navigate this resistance, it is essential for the management to proactively communicate the benefits of the CRM system, addressing concerns and emphasizing its positive impact on their daily workflows. By involving the sales team in the decision-making process and showcasing how the CRM aligns with their goals and objectives, resistance can transform into engagement. Additionally, providing comprehensive training and support during the initial stages of implementation helps ease the transition, allowing sales professionals to see the tangible advantages of the CRM system firsthand.

Communicating the benefits of CRM adoption for individual and team success is integral to fostering a positive and collaborative environment. Emphasizing the time-saving features, improved organization, and enhanced customer insights offered by the CRM system underscores its value for individual sales professionals. Highlighting how the CRM contributes to streamlined processes, efficient communication, and data-driven decision-making reinforces its impact on team success. By illustrating the potential for increased productivity, better-targeted sales efforts, and improved customer relationships, the management can instill a sense of ownership and enthusiasm among the sales team. Regularly sharing success stories and recognizing achievements facilitated by the CRM system further reinforces the positive outcomes, encouraging widespread adoption and integration into the team's daily operations.

Future Trends and Adaptability

Today's technology is not the leading edge tomorrow. Just as the "bag phone of the 1970's is outdated today, so too the great access to a CRM on the salesperson's smartphone may not be tomorrow's cutting-edge technology.

Just as the technology from your manufacturer in the equipment you sell is constantly changing, so too, will the technology change on what we today call CRM's. It will be your responsibility as sales manager to keep updated on what is current technology in your industry and how it impacts your function and your department.

Collaboration with Manufacturers and Suppliers

Every decision has consequences. Many OEM manufacturers have implemented a CRM to aid in salespeople getting all the data into a quotation correctly. If you chose to use that, you also are handing all of your customer information to your manufacturer. Could that eventually streamline you as a dealer/distributor out of the distribution pipeline? You will have to make that decision.

On the other hand, integrating with an OEM's customer/quoting database provides consistency, ensures that you are not quoting accounts that are possibly also being quoted by a neighboring dealer. And confirms between you and the manufacturer which dealer was quoting the customer first. Collaboration has it's values also.

Measuring Customer Satisfaction

Implementing CRM tools and processes to measure customer satisfaction is a strategic move that aligns with the customer-centric approach of the equipment industry. These tools can encompass surveys, feedback forms, and performance analytics integrated into the CRM system. By systematically gauging customer satisfaction, dealerships gain valuable insights into the strengths and weaknesses of their service delivery and sales process. Establishing key performance indicators (KPIs) related to customer satisfaction allows for the quantification of success and areas that may require improvement. This data-driven approach not only provides a clear understanding of customer sentiment but also serves as a foundation for refining CRM strategies to better meet customer expectations.

Utilizing feedback to refine CRM strategies for enhanced customer relationships is a dynamic and iterative process. The insights gathered from customer feedback within the CRM system become a catalyst for strategic adjustments. Identifying patterns and trends allows dealerships to address recurring issues promptly and capitalize on successful practices. The integration of feedback loops directly into the CRM workflow ensures a continuous improvement cycle. Sales teams can leverage this information to personalize interactions, anticipate customer needs, and enhance overall satisfaction. By actively involving the sales team in the analysis of customer feedback, organizations create a culture of responsiveness and adaptability. This iterative refinement process not only fortifies customer relationships but also positions the business to stay agile in a competitive market, ensuring that CRM strategies evolve to meet the ever-changing needs of the customer base.

Leveraging Customer Data for personal sales approaches

Customer Segmentation:

Segmentation	High	Medium	Low
A			
B			
C			
D			

We discussed segmenting and prioritizing your customers earlier in the book. Your CRM system can aid in maintaining and updating this. It also helps in analyzing your assignment of accounts to salespeople. Don't forget that you also can use the CRM system to track customer purchasing patterns and identify travel time for salespeople from one account to the next.

You want to store this information about your customer & prospect accounts in your CRM. It should be reviewed at least annually. Some customers that were a C have grown and are now a B level account, and some people that were low priority are now medium.

Personalized Communication:

Your CRM should include the ability to receive and send emails (even better if it can handle SMS text messaging, also). This should then assist you in automating some of your marketing, while still customizing your messages with customer name, company, location, etc. Doing this you can tailor messages, offers, and interactions based on the specific needs and preferences of each customer.

Beyond "Dear <<First_Name>>" you should involve someone in your organization who can write messages that bring personal information into your message much deeper in the content. Consider the following example:

Subject: Personalized Offer Just for You, [First_name]!

Dear [First_name],

I hope this email finds you well. As someone who values the quality and performance of [Brand] equipment, we thought you'd appreciate an exclusive offer tailored just for you.

We noticed that your last purchase with us was the [Last_Product_Purchased]. We trust it has been serving you reliably, and we're delighted to see you've chosen [Company] for your equipment needs.

To express our gratitude for your continued trust in .....

Even this example is still very commercial, and you should develop your own style and make the emails or text messages more personal and custom. But I wanted you to see the idea of using more than merely the customer's first name in a customized communication.

Historical Purchase Data:

Many customers purchase certain types of equipment in the same style from one purchase to another, but they might have a purchasing cycle. Some equipment is depreciated in a 5 or 7 year accounting cycle. Many customers recognize that the equipment also has lost the new technology edge within that time period, so they might be repurchasing new equipment with current cutting-edge technology in that cycle also.

If your CRM includes the equipment owned, purchased, rented or leased by a customer, then you should also be able to pull the equipment that is due to be "repurchased" by a customer in a certain purchase cycle. Those should be target accounts you begin working on 6-12 months ahead of their scheduled replacement point. Also if it's a lease, or financed, you should know what that target replacement point is going to be. That date should be in the equipment record, and salespeople should be using it to organize their efforts.

Creating a customer purchase timeline from information stored in your CRM (or ERP) could also aid your sales staff in identifying potential replacement purchasing prospects.

Service and Maintenance Insights:

No salesperson should ever think of going into a prospect to quote new equipment without having already analyzed the history, service costs and operator activities with the current equipment. Without knowing the customer's experience, expenses and pain points your deal is very likely to die before you write your quotation.

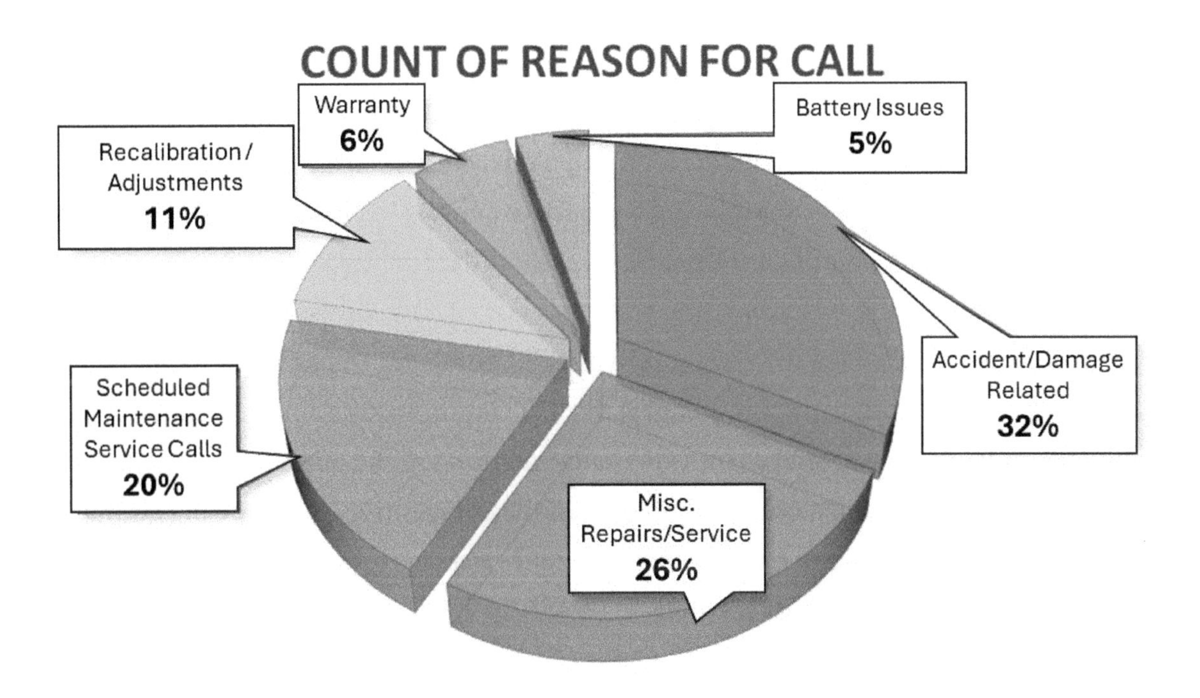

Whether the salespeople obtain their information from your ERP or from the CRM, they should also be looking for the service repair work that has occurred for this equipment. Recommended categories of analysis of the service works could be: Scheduled Maintenance, Warranty Work, Normal Wear& Tear, and Customer/Operator Abuse. The illustration chart should assist the salesperson in explaining the maintenance cost of the unit they are attempting to replace. If over the last five years the customer's largest maintenance cost has been Accident/Damage, then the point is, that is not a maintenance cost related to the equipment as much as to the environment it is used in or the careless operators using it.

The CRM adds the ability for allied (or related product sales) add-ons in addition to repairs and maintenance upsells. Higher level PMs is another good thing to track, and conversion rate of them quoted.

This same process should be something your service department and Aftermarket Sales staff are using regularly with major accounts. Identifying what is causing the Accident/Damage expenses which are preventable can save the customer money. This can translate to customer satisfaction and retention. But since this book is about sales management, we'll leave that discussion for another publication.

Follow-Up and Engagement:

A pivotal aspect of building enduring customer relationships and expanding the customer base lies in the ability to stay connected and responsive. Timely follow-ups demonstrate commitment and attentiveness, showcasing a proactive approach that resonates positively with clients. Harnessing the power of Customer Relationship Management (CRM) systems becomes instrumental in this regard. By automating routine tasks, CRM systems ensure that no potential sales opportunity slips through the cracks, providing a systematic and efficient method to nurture leads and maintain continuous engagement. This automation not only saves valuable time but also enhances the overall client experience, reinforcing the salesperson's commitment to a professional and customer-centric approach. In the competitive landscape of equipment sales, the strategic integration of CRM systems becomes a cornerstone in fostering lasting client connections and fostering a robust clientele.

Training and Development:

Over time you will have success stories and illustrations of mistakes that salespeople have created in recording and maintaining data in the CRM. Use these for good training with your staff. The issue is not to embarrass anyone, but to illustrate that good use of a CRM leads to stronger sales, better customer satisfaction and customer retention.

Don't hesitate to involve your sales staff in helping you identify what the CRM has done to help focus their attention on sales opportunities they would not have noticed in the past. Or, what information was in the CRM that they were not paying attention to, and therefore lost sales they could have made if they had used it better.

If you have established goals and best practices for your salespeople, then using your CRM is a tool for your to analyze their participation in following your suggestions/requirement. You should be able to obtain reports on:

- their number of calls per day,
- their coverage of deals in their territory,
- their close rate,
- accountability
- tracking goals with a dashboard

- number of open quotes,
- length of time to close quotes,
- their basic sales cycle,
- etc.

Managing long-term relationships for repeat business.

Customer Lifecycle Understanding:

Just as each piece of equipment has a lifecycle from quotation to sales, to installation, to warranty service, to scheduled maintenance, to breakdown/repair, to replacement; so to customers/prospects have a lifecycle. You start with suspect, and you qualify them, then they are a prospect, you sell them something (maybe not your primary product) but you get your foot in the door, and then you begin selling your prime products to them. But have your salespeople identified all of the related products you have access to that this new account also purchases from various other vendors. You want to control all the possible spending of these accounts for any product you can provide.

Your CRM should be assisting you in moving these accounts from each stage of development and their lifecycle to the next. Your CRM system should help map out and manage each stage effectively.

Proactive Relationship Building:

When working with your high priority A and B accounts the CRM should facilitate a proactive relationship with your contacts in those accounts. While your salespeople are expected to be busy, the CRM should aid them in maintaining regular communication, showing a personalized touch and possibly anticipating customer needs if you have included many of the features we have discussed here.

Highlighting the role of CRM in facilitating proactive relationship building is essential for understanding how this technology transforms customer interactions. Through effective CRM use, dealerships can establish a foundation for regular communication, personalized outreach, and anticipation of customer needs.

CRM systems serve as a centralized hub for customer information, allowing sales teams to maintain a comprehensive view of interactions, preferences, and historical data. This enables regular communication by providing timely reminders for follow-ups, scheduled calls, and important milestones in the customer journey. Through automated alerts and notifications, the CRM ensures that no opportunity for engagement is missed, fostering a consistent and proactive approach to relationship building.

Personalized outreach becomes seamless with CRM tools that enable the segmentation of customer data. By categorizing customers based on their preferences, purchase history, and communication preferences, your sales teams can tailor their outreach strategies. CRM facilitates the creation of targeted marketing campaigns, personalized emails, and customized offers, enhancing the overall customer experience.

This personalized approach demonstrates a deep understanding of individual needs and preferences, strengthening the bond between the dealership and its customers.

Is this automatic with every CRM? NO! You and your sales team are going to need to input data and determine what will assist you in developing this strong relationship with your accounts. Then you must follow through on your process. Some processes are better than other, but your follow through is probably what makes one better than the other.

Anticipating customer needs is a key aspect of proactive relationship building, and CRM plays a pivotal role in this regard. By analyzing customer data and interactions, CRM systems generate valuable insights into behavioral patterns and emerging trends. Sales teams can leverage this information to predict customer needs, recommend relevant products or services, and address potential issues before they arise. With CRM-driven analytics, dealerships can stay ahead of customer expectations, fostering a proactive and responsive relationship-building strategy that goes beyond mere transactional interactions.

In essence, effective CRM use transforms customer relationships from reactive to proactive, creating a dynamic and personalized engagement model that builds loyalty and drives long-term success.

Predictive Analytics for Upselling and Cross-selling:

Predictive analytics within a CRM system is a potent tool for unlocking upselling and cross-selling opportunities by delving into customers' past purchasing behaviors. By meticulously analyzing historical data stored in the CRM, dealerships gain invaluable insights into patterns and trends that can illuminate future needs. For instance, if a customer consistently purchases construction equipment, the CRM's predictive analytics can anticipate when maintenance services or complementary tools might be needed. This proactive approach allows sales teams to strategically position upselling opportunities, offering customers tailored solutions before they even recognize the requirement themselves. This collection of history, and collective information from other customers could provide information for Full Maintenance Sales Contracts, PM or Scheduled Maintenance plans or downtime rental agreements all packaged with the original sale of the equipment. These additional sales products could make your deal stand out with target accounts.

LifeTime Value of a Customer

10 year Evaluation with		5 Year Purchase Cycle	
Equipment Purchase Value		$30,000	
Annual Service		10	Hours
Labor Billing Rate		$120.00	
Parts Value to Labor Value		50/50	

	Equipment	Service	Parts
1st year	$ 30,000	$ 1,200	$ 1,200
2nd year		$ 1,200	$ 1,200
3rd year		$ 1,200	$ 1,200
4th year		$ 1,200	$ 1,200
5th year		$ 1,200	$ 1,200
6th year	$ 30,000	$ 1,200	$ 1,200
7th year		$ 1,200	$ 1,200
8th year		$ 1,200	$ 1,200
9th year		$ 1,200	$ 1,200
10th year		$ 1,200	$ 1,200
Totals	**$ 60,000**	**$ 12,000**	**$ 12,000**
Profit Margin	8.00%	65.00%	35.00%
10 Yr Gross Profit	$ 4,800	$ 7,800	$ 4,200
Expected Net Profit	$ 720	$ 2,340	$ 840

Figure 1 This 10 Year Forklift Customer Illustration can demonstrate the lifetime customer value

The CRM helps identify demand and therefore which sales items to promote and when (it helps the sell as well as stocking side to buy in quantity and improve the GP as much as possible). There could be integration with parts ordering software to push items that need more turns or are overstocked in some dealerships .

To practically leverage CRM insights and boost the lifetime value of each customer, dealerships should focus on personalized recommendations. The CRM's segmentation capabilities enable the categorization of customers based on their preferences, buying history, and engagement patterns. Armed with this information, dealerships can employ targeted communication strategies, suggesting complementary products or services that align seamlessly with each customer's past purchases. For example, if a customer frequently buys agricultural machinery, the CRM can prompt your sales team to recommend compatible accessories or the latest models in the same product line, fostering a deeper connection with the customer and enhancing overall satisfaction.

Furthermore, dealerships can employ automated triggers and alerts embedded in the CRM to prompt timely engagement. If a customer's equipment is approaching the end of its lifespan, the CRM can generate alerts, enabling sales representatives to proactively recommend upgraded models or extended warranty packages. This dynamic use of predictive analytics ensures that dealerships not only meet current customer needs but also anticipate and fulfill future requirements, ultimately increasing the lifetime value of each customer and solidifying long-term relationships.

Automated Follow-Up and Engagement:

Automation plays a pivotal role in maintaining consistent follow-up and engagement within CRM systems, ensuring that dealerships can stay connected with their customers without manual oversight. CRM systems are equipped with automation features that can send timely reminders for periodic check-ins, service appointments, or personalized promotional offers. For instance, if a customer's equipment is due for routine maintenance, the CRM can automatically generate a service reminder, prompting the sales or service team to reach out proactively. This not only streamlines communication but also showcases a commitment to customer care, fostering a sense of reliability and trust.

Successful automated engagement strategies contribute significantly to strengthened long-term relationships. A prime example is personalized promotional offers triggered by the CRM based on a customer's purchase history. If a customer frequently buys a particular type of industrial equipment, the CRM can automate the delivery of exclusive discounts or tailored promotions for related accessories or upgrades. This targeted and automated approach not only enhances the customer's experience but also demonstrates a deep understanding of their preferences, cultivating a sense of loyalty and satisfaction. By leveraging automation in these strategic ways, dealerships can nurture enduring relationships with their customers, creating a win-win scenario where customers feel valued, and dealerships secure repeat business and customer advocacy.

Feedback Loops and Continuous Improvement:

Feedback loops in CRM systems are instrumental for fostering continuous improvement in products, services, and overall customer satisfaction. By actively seeking and collecting feedback from customers through CRM channels, dealerships gain valuable insights into their strengths and areas that require enhancement. This iterative process allows companies to adapt swiftly to changing customer preferences, market trends, and emerging needs. A well-established feedback loop within a CRM system creates a dynamic and responsive environment where customer opinions serve as a catalyst for strategic adjustments, contributing to the ongoing evolution of products and services.

Several dealerships have successfully implemented changes based on customer feedback gathered through CRM systems, exemplifying the real-world impact of feedback loops. For instance, a manufacturing company utilizing CRM feedback identified a recurring issue with the usability of a particular industrial tool. By analyzing the feedback trends, the company revamped the tool's design, addressing user concerns and significantly improving functionality. This adjustment not only resolved customer pain points but also resulted in increased customer satisfaction and a boost in product sales. Another example involves an e-commerce platform that used CRM feedback to refine its customer service processes. By collating feedback on response times, issue resolution, and overall service quality, the platform implemented targeted training programs for its support team, leading to a substantial improvement in customer satisfaction ratings and a reduction in customer complaints.

Consider taking customer surveys / 360 reviews and posting results in CRM to see if you can improve any goal metrics in customer experience. It can also integrate warranty status and pending campaigns status (internally helping prioritize for staff) and notifications (external for customers to schedule or communicate with dealership)

These stories underscore the pivotal role of feedback loops in CRM systems, showcasing how dealerships that actively seek and leverage customer feedback can drive positive change, enhance customer experiences, and ultimately fortify their competitive position in the market.

Personalized Customer Service:

CRM data serves as a goldmine for providing personalized customer service, allowing equipment dealerships to tailor their support based on individual customer needs and preferences. Moreover, CRM data can help dealerships proactively address issues by tracking a customer's historical interactions and resolutions, enabling faster and more effective problem resolution. Dealerships that excel in utilizing CRM data for personalized customer service often find themselves not just meeting expectations but exceeding them by going the extra mile to anticipate and fulfill unique customer needs.

Exceptional personalized service contributes significantly to building lasting relationships and fostering customer loyalty. Customers appreciate dealerships that understand their preferences, anticipate their needs, and provide tailored solutions. In the context of equipment dealerships, going beyond transactional interactions to offer personalized service creates a sense of trust and loyalty. For instance, a dealership that uses CRM data to remember a customer's equipment preferences, service history, and communication preferences can seamlessly offer a personalized experience during every interaction. This, in turn, leads to increased customer satisfaction, repeat business, and positive word-of-mouth referrals. In the competitive landscape of the equipment industry, personalized service not only sets dealerships apart but also cements enduring relationships, contributing to long-term customer loyalty. Personal follow up with a customer could also include knowing when their birthday is, their sports preferences, items about their family, when their last promotion was, who their boss is, etc. When you are assigned hundreds of accounts having something that keeps track of all of this information about a customer can be very helpful.

Whenever individuals were slated for a follow-up meeting with Franklin D. Roosevelt, James Farley (Roosevelt's campaign manager, and later Postmaster General) would meticulously examine their records. This enabled Roosevelt to engage with them once more with a comprehensive understanding of details like their spouse's identity, the names and ages of their children, and any other pertinent information gleaned from prior meetings or additional insights thoughtfully added to the file by Farley. The impact was both profound and personal. Your CRM is capable of doing the same thing for you.

In conclusion, the effective use of CRM data is a cornerstone for delivering personalized customer service in equipment dealerships. From tailoring support to resolving issues promptly, CRM empowers dealerships to cater to individual customer needs, fostering loyalty and long-lasting relationships. As dealerships continue to harness the power of CRM, they position themselves to not only meet but exceed customer expectations, ultimately driving sustained success in the ever-evolving landscape of the equipment industry.

10. Recruiting and Training

Various methodologies and techniques can be utilized to improve managerial effectiveness with existing employees. However, addressing performance challenges may not always require the introduction of new techniques for current employees but could involve considering new hires. Additionally, as employees depart or the business expands, the need for new hires becomes evident.

Considering that staffing decisions have lasting implications, it becomes crucial to thoroughly examine the recruiting and selection process, particularly the criteria guiding these decisions. Subsequently, attention can be directed toward the effective training of new hires.

The central activities in this process revolve around communication and decision-making. The interviewer collects information and forms impressions to forecast the candidate's future performance in the vacant position. The primary objectives of this unit are to counteract poor interview habits, provide rational motives for making hiring decisions, present a model to follow, and establish the foundation for implementing correct interviewing skills and techniques.

While it is impossible to predict with absolute certainty how a candidate will perform in a complex position based on a 30 to 60-minute interview, effective practices can yield crucial impressions and a relative indication of performance. Consequently, it is essential for the interviewer to possess a comprehensive understanding of the entire process and adopt a systematic approach to recruiting and selecting to ensure the making of successful choices.

Dealing with Stereotypes

Managers should be mindful of specific stereotypes and attitudes that influence their decision-making. Some of these stereotypes are entirely valid and simply offer a convenient way to navigate our impressions. For instance, if you are seeking tax advice, you might stereotypically opt for a Chartered Accountant, while someone else may choose a tax attorney. Both choices are valid but represent stereotypical responses.

However, other stereotypes may not accurately reflect the "actual" credentials of the person (job candidate), and it is essential to counteract the limitations they impose on us. Managers need to look beyond stereotypes to address the real issues when making a hiring decision and resist the temptation to take the easy shortcuts that stereotyping provides. Whenever feasible, the focus should be on identifying qualities in a candidate that are job-related and measurable. Candidates should always be evaluated against the Job Model, which represents the qualities desired in the "IDEAL" candidates for the position in question.

The Job Model

Essentially, a job should be organized based on the essential components inherent to the role. A job description constitutes a fundamental aspect of the job model and should be established before a new hire accumulates enough experience to independently generate it, a common scenario. If a new job cannot be outlined through a job description beforehand, it raises the crucial question of whether the job has been thoroughly conceptualized.

All positions require knowledge and technical skills—information and acquired abilities that candidates must possess to meet the minimum standards required for the job. Closely linked to these prerequisites are the performance factors or measurable outcomes that enable us to evaluate how effectively the specific tasks associated with the job are performed.

Ultimately, the personal characteristics relevant to the successful execution of the job must be distinctly identified. The subsequent depiction illustrates the Job Model as a sequence of discernible steps.

The Job Model

WHAT DOES THE JOB ENTAIL?

(ex. long hours, demanding pace, ability to accept rejection, self-starter)

WHAT SKILLS, KNOWLEDGE, TRAITS ARE NEEDED?

(ex. high energy level, persistence, empathy)

WHAT EVIDENCE SUGGESTS THIS SKILL, KNOWLEDGE, TRAIT IS PRESENT?

(prior success, presence, interview)

QUESTIONS TO EVOKE THIS DATA

(Describe your management approach. How do you handle price objections?)

INFORMATION FROM APPLICANT

EVALUATING THE DATA

DECISION (hire or not)

Some key points that you should carefully consider when using the job model are as follows:

Key Points:

1. People tend to lean towards hiring individuals who share similar traits with them.
2. Pinpointing the most qualified candidate becomes difficult without a CLEAR grasp of the job requirements.
3. Each criterion specified in the job model should have a direct relevance to the job at hand.
4. Being mindful of legal implications is crucial; a thorough review of relevant laws is a necessity.
5. After crafting the job model, the interviewer develops questions to be asked to EACH candidate, concentrating on areas crucial to the job model rather than questions solely driven by the resume.

Screening Candidates

An interview functions as an organized, behavioral sampling of a candidate, enabling the formulation of conclusions. This process typically involves two sets of questions.

1. The structured interview, which consists of a predefined set of written questions entirely guided by the job model, is administered to all candidates (as mentioned earlier).
2. Candidate-driven questions arise from a thorough examination of preliminary information, enabling the creation of hypotheses that require verification during the

interview. These questions focus on areas of uncertainty associated with the job model, originating from.

- Resume screening
- Phone screening
- Job application form
- Insights from an employee familiar with the candidate

These questions are introduced alongside those designed for the job model but are customized to the unique characteristics of each candidate. When uncertainty arises from resume, phone, or other screening methods, it represents a hypothesis formed solely based on the individual candidate's distinctive attributes and history, as opposed to questions influenced by the job model. Here are some areas to examine when screening a resume: unexplained gaps in resume background.

- lack of detail regarding experience
- the meaning of job titles
- salary history

It's essential to underscore that areas of investigation can be either favorable or unfavorable. The crucial factor is the existing lack of certainty — at this point, we lack knowledge! The resume introduces certain uncertainties that require further scrutiny during the interview. It is crucial to avoid making premature judgments about the candidate.

There might be entirely valid explanations for the areas of investigation you emphasize. These explanations could, in fact, offer very positive insights. However, clarity on these matters only arises through effective exploration during the interview. **A final reminder — avoid conducting interviews with candidates on short notice or when unprepared.**

The Four Types of Questioning Techniques

1. Open-ended questions are formulated to encourage the candidate to elaborate on a specific area. For instance, "Elaborate on your achievements in sales during your most recent role."

2. Closed-ended questions seek to extract precise facts, typically prompting a yes/no response. They are valuable for verifying information or attitudes. For example, "Did you also oversee allied products in your previous position?" (This should then lead to an open-ended question.)
3. Probes serve the purpose of verifying or supplementing existing information, offering clarification on facts or attitudes.
4. The utilization of silence is a technique that induces tension, aiming to prompt a more detailed response to open-ended or probing questions. Employing operant conditioning, it may involve reinforcing responses like, "Yes, good, please continue."

5. Asking for More Information (Probes)

1. Could you elaborate on your statement?
2. I would like to delve deeper into your perspective.
3. I'm unclear about your intentions. Can you offer more clarity?
4. What brings you to hold that specific viewpoint?
5. Could you offer further details on that particular point?
6. Can you provide me with additional information on that?
7. Would you offer a more detailed description of that?
8. Are there other factors shaping your perspective?
9. Employing a moment of silence

Criteria for a "Good" Question

1. Endures scrutiny regarding the question "Why is this question pertinent?"
2. Clearly fulfills its intended purpose
3. Harmonizes with a methodical approach
4. Aims to draw comparisons and distinctions
5. Encourages transparent communication
6. Focuses on specific categories of information
7. Steers clear of being suggestive or leading
8. Exhibits attentive listening
9. Upholds a non-threatening demeanor

Interview Questions

Warm-Up Questions

1. What drove you to apply for this role?
2. How did you discover information about this job opportunity?
3. Could you offer a brief overview of your professional history and educational background?
4. In your previous (sales) positions, what kind of supervision did you encounter?
5. Can you recall one or two significant setbacks you faced in your professional journey?
6. What inspired you to pursue a career in sales?
7. What influenced your decision to depart from your current position? (Alternatively, why did you leave your previous position?)
8. What qualities do you value in your colleagues, and what is the rationale behind your preference?
9. Among all the roles you've undertaken, which one did you find most satisfying?
10. What type of organizational environment do you find most conducive to your work?
11. How does this job align with your broader career objectives?
12. Share details about a novel idea or technique you developed in a prior role that you take pride in.

Education

1. What distinctive aspects of your education or training have prepared you for this role?
2. Narrate the initial training you underwent in your last position. Also, delve into any ongoing training you received and evaluate the impact of these training experiences.
3. Contemplate how your education or training has elevated your performance in past roles.
4. From your educational background, which experiences have been most advantageous in your professional responsibilities?
5. If you were to attain this position, in which areas would you seek additional training?

Career Goals

1. Career Goals Inquiry:

a. Elaborate on your professional aspirations.

b. Outline the role you foresee for yourself in five years.

c. Justify why this career objective aligns with your strengths.

d. Explain how achieving this position contributes to your broader career goal.

2. Accomplishments & Ambitions:

a. Share your primary objectives upon securing this role.

3. Potential Departure Factors:

a. Identify circumstances that might lead you to contemplate leaving.

4. Salesperson Perception:

a. Define your perception of the qualities embodied by a successful salesperson.

5. Alternate Profession Scenario:

a. Envision an alternative career if sales were not your focus.

Job Performance

1. Self-Reflection on Strengths and Weaknesses:

a. Highlight your noteworthy strengths.

b. Identify areas you acknowledge for improvement.

2. Supervisor Evaluation Inquiry:

a. Discuss your recent supervisor's evaluation, encompassing both strengths and weaknesses.

3. Performance Versus Quota Analysis:

a. Provide specific details on your performance compared to quota in the last two years.

4. Quota Setting and Perception:
a. Explore how quotas were established, your sentiments toward them, and their positive or negative aspects.
5. Approach to Addressing Performance Issues:
a. Describe your actions when confronted with job performance challenges, offering a specific example.
6. Personal Perspective on Sales Role:
a. Share your sentiments regarding being a salesperson.
7. Enjoyment in Sales:
a. Discuss what aspects of selling you find most enjoyable.
8. Challenges in Sales:
a. Identify aspects of selling that you find less favorable.

Absenteeism

1. Absence and Time Off Inquiry:
a. Can you indicate the number of days you were not present last year?
b. What was the reason for your absence?
c. Elaborate on your most recent extended absence (beyond two or three days).
d. Discuss the one preceding the last extended absence.
2. Approach to Addressing Absenteeism:
a. Share your viewpoint on how issues related to absenteeism should be handled.

Salary and Benefits

1. Previous Compensation Structure:
a. Expand on the details of the compensation package from your previous role.
2. Attitude Toward Commission:
a. Express your feelings about a commission-based compensation structure.
3. Earnings Overview:
a. Offer insights into your earnings over the last few years, aligning with the performance discussed earlier.
4. Importance of Benefits:

a. Discuss the importance you place on various job benefits.
5. Compensation Self-Reflection:
a. Compare your perceived worth with the compensation received in your past positions.

Sales Skills Questions

Salesmanship

1. Share details of your most challenging sales experience.
2. Outline your approach to the initial 30 days of establishing new accounts.
3. Respond to a sales scenario: In your previous role, you sold ____. I'll take on the role of the buyer. I acknowledge your product's quality, but I can acquire brand X for 20% less.
4. From your perspective, what does the role of selling entail?
5. What attributes do you believe I am seeking in a salesperson?
6. If you were in my position, what qualities would you look for in a candidate for this role?
7. Present hypothetical situations and inquire about the candidate's problem-solving approach.
8. In your opinion, how should a salesperson present themselves to prospects and customers?
9. Explain your process for qualifying a prospect. Specifically, highlight the crucial information required before progressing in the sales process and the questions you ask to obtain this information.
10. In the last sale that you lost (or won), how extensive was your involvement?
11. How would you present your current product to a prospect?
12. Describe how you organize your prospect and customer files.
13. Explain your prospect follow-up system.
14. What items do you typically carry in your briefcase when visiting a prospect? What resources do you keep in your car?

15. How do you feel about a computerized call reporting system?
16. What information about your daily activities should management be aware of to fulfill their responsibilities effectively?

Knowledge and Utilization of Company Resources

1. Which company resources or services did you most frequently utilize?
2. Describe the training or information you received regarding these resources.
3. How do colleagues typically seek your assistance as a resource?
4. With whom do you collaborate to achieve your goals?
5. When faced with a sales problem you cannot solve, what is your approach?
6. Which departments have proven to be the most supportive in your experience?
7. Have you ever encountered an ethical dilemma in your role as a salesperson?
8. In what aspects of your current job do you believe you make personal sacrifices?
9. Can you suggest any changes to your company's existing policies or procedures that would enhance your effectiveness as a salesperson?
10. What technical publications do you regularly read?
11. Pose a technical question related to current events in the industry to the candidate.

Questions for Decision Making

Problem Solving and Creativity

Decisiveness

1. Decision-Making Style:

a. Would you characterize yourself as thoughtful and analytical, or do you generally make quick decisions? Provide an example.

2. Recent Challenging Decision:

a. Reflect on the most challenging decision you've made in the past six months. What factors made it particularly difficult?

3. Handling Uncertainty:

a. When confronted with uncertainty about a decision, what approach do you typically adopt?

4. Career-Impacting Decisions:

a. How do you approach the process of making substantial decisions that have an impact on your career?

5. Resolution of Major Problems:

a. Share details about the last significant problem you encountered. What steps did you take to address and resolve it?

Problem Analysis

1. Problem Awareness:

a. In sales, remaining vigilant to potential problems is essential. How do you ensure you stay tuned to possible issues?

2. Toughest Sales Problems:

a. From your perspective, what are the most formidable challenges that salespeople often face? Can you provide an example?

3. Handling Recent Challenges:

a. Reflect on the most significant problem you've encountered in the past six months. How did you navigate and resolve it?

4. Approaching Complex Problems:

a. When confronted with a intricate problem, do you follow a specific procedure? What elements do you consider most important, and why?

5. Information Sources for Problem Awareness:

a. How do you leverage various sources of information to stay informed about potential issues with your customers and prospects?

6. Anticipating Market Challenges:

a. Looking ahead, what do you foresee as the major challenges in your market over the next five years?

7. Dealing with Product Issues:
a. When a product encounters challenges, what steps do you take to address and rectify the situation?

Creativity

1. Implications of a Four-Day Work Week:
a. If the standard becomes a four-day work week, what do you anticipate as the general implications or impact on your outcomes?
2. Pinnacle of Creativity:
a. Contemplate the most creative thing you've done. What distinguished that particular achievement?
3. Circumstances Fostering Creativity:
a. Under what circumstances do you find yourself most creative? Share an experience that illustrates this.
4. Truly Creative Work Experience:
a. In your work history, can you identify an instance where you undertook something you consider genuinely creative?
5. Involvement in Organizations:
a. Have you played a role in founding a business or civic organization? Share your experience and contributions.
6. Innovative Problem-Solving:
a. Recall a situation where conventional solutions failed, and you devised new ones. Please elaborate on this problem-solving experience.

7. Creative Accomplishments and Satisfaction:

8. Of all your creative accomplishments, whether significant or minor, work-related or personal, which one brought you the most satisfaction?

9. Recent Problem-Solving Challenges:

a. What kinds of problems have people recently sought your assistance in solving? Provide insight into your devised solutions.

Work Standards

1. Standards of Success:

a. Can you express the criteria that define success in your role?

2. Recognition Practices:

a. Provide insights into how you acknowledge and reward individuals who exceed work standards.

3. Employee Dismissal Criteria:

a. Under what conditions would you contemplate terminating an employee?

4. Compromise and Assistance:

a. To what extent are you willing to adjust your standards to assist someone?

5. Definition of a Good Job:

a. How do you characterize a job well done in your position, and what influenced this definition?

6. Key Factors in Subordinate Performance:

a. When assessing a subordinate's performance, what factors or traits hold the most significance for you?

7. Contribution to Company Profitability:

a. Identify the most crucial contribution you believe you can make to enhance the long-term profitability of the company.

8. Personal Productivity Potential:

a. If collaboration, optimal individual performance, and the elimination of inefficiencies were realized, how much could you increase your personal productivity?

9. Satisfaction with Organizational Performance:

a. Are you content with the overall performance of your organization?

Conducting the Interview

An interview, similar to any interpersonal interaction, follows a particular pattern that carries significance. Essentially, an interview is a condensed version of interpersonal engagement, comprising three distinct parts:

The Opening -- Establishing Rapport/Climate:

The initiation of the interview establishes the overall atmosphere. The interviewer's objective is to foster an environment conducive to open information sharing. It is essential to bring the candidate to a reasonable anxiety level. The emphasis is on comprehending how individuals will perform on the job rather than evaluating them solely on their interview skills.

The Body -- Questioning and Probing:

At the heart of the interview, this phase is designed to gather information that can predict future job performance. Questions asked should be influenced by both the job model and the candidate. Here is a procedural guide for the interviewer during this segment of the interview:

Ensure Privacy

Utilize Appropriate Questioning Techniques:

1. Open-Ended: Encourage the candidate to elaborate on specific areas. Example: "Elaborate on your approach to handling challenging situations in previous roles."
2. Close-Ended: Seek precise facts, often resulting in yes/no responses. Example: "Did you achieve your sales targets in your last position?"
3. Probes: Clarify or supplement existing information. Example: "Can you provide more insight into how you managed team conflicts in your previous job?"
4. Silence: Used strategically to prompt more comprehensive responses, especially after open-ended or probing questions. Example: "Take your time. I'm interested in hearing your thoughts."
5. Avoid Leading Questions: Steer clear of questions that may influence or guide the candidate's responses.

Take Detailed Notes: - Facilitates recall of the candidate's responses and assists in accurate comparison with the job model.

Aids Memory Retention: - Assists in remembering crucial details about the candidate's experiences and qualifications.

Ensures Accurate Job Model Comparison: - Enables a precise evaluation by aligning the candidate's responses with the established job model. (Hiring managers should explain in advance how they will be conducting the interview and explain that they will be taking notes to keep a record of the important points that are made during their conversation.)

Listen

- **Discern Implicit Meanings:** - Attend to subtle nuances and unspoken messages conveyed by the candidate.
- **Assess the Weight of Points:** - Evaluate the importance of the information presented by the candidate.
- **Periodic Review of Information:** - Take moments to contemplate the content shared during the interview.
- **Caution with Emotional Responses:** - Exercise caution when responding to emotionally charged words, ensuring a measured approach.
- **Awareness of Biases:** - Be mindful of personal biases that may impact your interpretation of the candidate's responses.
- **Identify Hidden Situations:** - Listen for undisclosed circumstances that may influence the candidate's suitability.
- **Avoid Assumptions:** - Refrain from making assumptions without sufficient evidence.
- **Balanced Note-Taking:** - Strike a balance between effective note-taking and active listening to grasp the full context.
- **Minimize Distractions:** - Reduce disruptions through thorough planning, allowing for focused attention.
- **80/20 Principle:** - Recognize the crucial 20% of information that provides 80% of the candidate's suitability insights.
- **Repetition:** - Reinforce key points to enhance understanding and ensure clarity.

- **Paraphrasing:** - Summarize or rephrase information to confirm comprehension and convey engagement.

Feedback of Feeling (Empathy):

Show empathy by recognizing and comprehending the emotional elements of the candidate's story.

Notice Non-Verbal Indications: - Be attentive to non-verbal cues that might signify increased anxiety in the candidate.

Evaluate the Suitability of Anxiety: - Assess whether the observed anxiety corresponds with the interview context or if it indicates underlying issues related to the nature of the questions posed.

Closing the Interview -- End the Interview on a Positive Note; Boosting Self-Esteem

Facilitate Candidate's Inquiries: - Allow the candidate a chance to raise any lingering questions.

Summarize Critical Aspects: - Review vital information and communicate any required steps for the candidate to take.

Communicate Decision Timeline:- Clarify when the decision will be made, ensuring transparency in the process.

Express Appreciation:- Convey gratitude to the candidate for their time and active participation.

Boost Confidence:- Provide positive reinforcement to bolster the candidate's confidence.

Escort from Premises:- Personally accompany the candidate from your office to the designated area, demonstrating professionalism and courtesy.

After The Interview: Evaluating Data

Promptly review the notes you've taken and reassess your impressions of the candidate. Develop assumptions about the candidate's characteristics based on the gathered information and its relevance to the job model. In some instances, additional managers may have participated in the interview process. If that's the case, compare your notes with theirs, and collectively evaluate how well the candidate aligns with the job model. If needed, reach out to the candidate for clarification on certain points. Ultimately, make a decision on whether to proceed with a second interview, extend a job offer, or decline the candidate.

Follow Up Interviews

Upon completing initial interviews to identify candidates aligned with the job model, it's crucial to conduct follow-up interviews to evaluate their compatibility with your organization's culture. Review selected questions from the first interview, with a focus on eliciting deeper feelings from the candidates. For example, inquire about their sentiments toward the sales profession or the ethical standards they consider appropriate in a highly competitive business.

Typically, this follow-up interview occurs at the dealership and involves the candidate along with one or two dealership representatives. Before extending the final job offer, seasoned managers often arrange a concluding interview with both the candidate and their spouse. This meeting commonly takes place in a social environment, such as a dinner at a reputable restaurant. This setting offers a different perspective on the candidate, and the spouse's input may reveal valuable insights.

An important aspect of this final interview is assessing the candidate's understanding and support in their home life. Specific questions directed to the spouse can cover topics like their feelings about the position, compensation, future prospects, the dealership, and more. Beyond evaluating the candidate, this interview serves to communicate the high expectations for commitment and performance. It also reinforces the cultural value of balancing career and family, a crucial element for employee integration.

Many managers have found the final interview with both the candidate and spouse to be enlightening and beneficial in gaining a comprehensive understanding.

Summary

The format and details presented here might appear extensive to some, but they are necessary for making informed and effective hiring decisions. Although it requires time and may involve some costs, the expense incurred from suboptimal hiring practices and trial-and-error choices is considerably higher.

Extra Material:

Job Description	**Sales Representative**
Position Specifics:	
Department:	Sales
Reports To:	Store Manager, Sales Manager, or Dealer Principal
Supervises:	No One
Purpose:	
	Sells new and used equipment to new and existing customers.
Responsibilities:	
	○ Represents the company for the sale of equipment to customers in a defined sales area (or specified listing of assigned accounts). ○ Maintains current product knowledge on features and benefits of all equipment potentially saleable by the dealership. ○ Monitors competitive activity/products and timely communicates to management accordingly. ○ Maintains all customer information in assigned territory for sales management. ○ Knows and follows a defined sales process ○ Maintains assigned company vehicles and equipment. ○ Assists with the preparation and execution of customer events. ○ Conducts new equipment demonstrations. ○ Monitors trends in customer's business activities and timely communicates to management. ○ Maintains current knowledge of financing options to assist customers with securing the purchase of new and used equipment. ○ Attends applicable sales training events/seminars. ○ May maintain current knowledge of used equipment values and ability to evaluate properly for trading purposes.

Requirements:	<ul><li>__+ years of equipment sales experience</li><li>Knowledge of equipment and industry or operational practices preferred</li><li>Ability to use standard desktop, load applications such as Microsoft Office and internet functions.</li><li>Ability to work flexible hours.</li><li>Excellent customer relationship skills.</li><li>Ability to analyze and interpret basic sales reports.</li><li>High School Diploma or equivalent work experience.</li></ul>

Job Description **Sales Manager**	
Position Specifics:	
Department:	Sales
Reports To:	General Manager, CEO, or Dealer Principal
Supervises:	Salespeople, Sales Specialists, Used Equipment Manager, and Sales Support Staff
Purpose:	
	Manages sales functions for the entire dealership including the implementation of a defined sales process, coaching, and developing sales professionals. Responsible for all sales metrics for the dealership. Hires, retains, and effectively engages department personnel
Responsibilities:	
	o Manages and coaches sales professionals to implement the sales process. o Creates development plans for sales professionals which include identifying training needs. o Develops and executes the Sales Department metrics and goals. o Implements a consistent sales process that drives optimal financial, market and customer performance. o Ensures the sales document process is established and followed by all sales team members. o Creates and executes an effective equipment marketing strategy. o Manages new complete goods inventory which includes maintaining proper inventory levels and order program utilization. o Identifies and executes best practices throughout the sales department.

	o Develops and implements incentives plans for sales team and customers. o Develops the Sales Department business plan and reviews progress regularly. o Works with Parts and Service Managers or the Corporate Aftermarket Manager to promote customer satisfaction. o Manages recruiting, staffing and employee development activities for employees reporting to this position. o Manages sales department equipment including vehicles and sales office equipment. May manage used equipment processes and inventory
Requirements:	o 3+ years of equipment sales experience o Ability to teach and coach sales professionals on selling techniques and sales processes. o Experience leading others o Familiar with John Deere and competitive products o Ability to use Deere sales computer applications and tools. o Ability to use software applications such as Microsoft Office and Deere systems. o Ability to analyze and interpret internal reports. o High School Diploma or equivalent work experience Associate or Bachelor's Degree in business or marketing preferred

While the two previous job descriptions are interesting, in some fashion they said "are you a good potential, and will you play nice with other departments." What we see consistently missing is the following specifications for the job. The intent of these benchmarks is to be concrete, measurable benchmarks of accomplishment in the job. Without these specifics attached to the Job Description, there is no objective measurement of accomplishment.

Additionally, have you looked on Salary.com or other compensation studies or sites to determine the pay range for these positions in your industry and in your local geography?

Benchmarks:	**Sales Manager**	
Benchmarks of Performance	**Revenue Growth or Market Share**	Annual Market Share Percentage of ____% Revenue Growth of ____% over Last Year
	Financial Performance	Gross Profit Percentage of ____% Net Profit Percentage of ____%
	Employee Productivity	Annual Gross Profit per Salesperson of $_____,_____
	Asset Management	New Equipment turns of _____x Used Equipment Turns of _____x
	Customer Satisfaction	Customer satisfaction and **expects an 85% target**
Compensation	**Method of Pay**	☑ Salary ☐ Hourly ☐ Commission
	Pay Range:	$XX,000 - $XXX,000 per year
	Vacation Eligibility	Yes – As Outlined in the Company Employee Manual
	Incentive Options:	Yes, Be specific

Benchmarks:	**Salesperson**	
Benchmarks of Performance	**Revenue Growth or Market Share**	Annual Market Share Percentage of ____% Revenue Growth of ____% over Last Year
	Financial Performance	Average Monthly Gross Profit Dollars $20,000+
	Employee Productivity	Target Annual Gross Profit Percentage _____%
	Asset Management	Number of New Unit Sales ______ Number of Used Equipment Units Sold _____x
	Customer Satisfaction	Customer satisfaction and **expects an 85% target**
Compensation	**Method of Pay**	☐ Salary ☐ Hourly ☐ Commission
	Pay Range:	$XX,000 - $XXX,000 per year
	Vacation Eligibility	Yes – As Outlined in the Company Employee Manual
	Incentive Options:	Yes, Be specific

Salesperson Breakeven Analysis

SALESPERSON COSTS

Salary & Benefits			% of Total	
Base Salary	$	30,000	32%	6 month forgivable draw
Benefits	$	3,600	4%	
Variable Compensation	$	60,000	64%	25.0%
Total Compensation	$	93,600		Commission as % of gross margin see margin and sales below
Resources				
Vehicle/Car Allowance	$	8,000		Fuel & Car
Communications/Phone	$	1,200		Computer & Phone
Total Resources	$	9,200		
Total Annual Costs of Salesperson	$	102,800		
BREAK EVEN ANALYSIS				
Gross Margin % for Complete Goods (Rolling 12 Months)		10.0%		
Breakeven Sales Required	$	1,030,000		
Avg Monthly Sales @ Breakeven	$	85,833		
POTENTIAL GAIN IN GROSS MARGIN				
Estimated Sales per Salesperson	$	2,400,000		
Dealer Net Gain Gross Margin	$	137,000		TIP (don'tforget that your variable compensation may impact this figure if it changes

This cost analysis is merely an illustration of what you might consider in determining compensation levels.

11. Sales Department Culture Issues

Nurturing a Healthy Sales Department Culture

Fostering a positive culture within a sales department is not just an added bonus but a fundamental element for achieving lasting success in the competitive realm of equipment dealership sales. This kind of culture goes much beyond individual accomplishments or hitting sales targets. It creates an environment where teamwork, excitement, and a unified pursuit of excellence are nurtured. In such an atmosphere, sales team members feel a sense of purpose and belonging, leading to increased motivation and job satisfaction. This, in turn, boosts productivity and makes the workplace more enjoyable. Such a positive environment is also key to attracting and retaining the best talent, as people are naturally drawn to workplaces that recognize and support their professional growth.

The link between a thriving sales department culture and improved sales performance is deep and multi-dimensional. A culture focused on continuous learning and development equips sales professionals with the necessary skills and knowledge to effectively navigate the industrial equipment market. When team members feel appreciated and supported, they tend to put in extra effort for their clients, leading to better customer satisfaction and loyalty. Moreover, a healthy culture encourages open communication, allowing the sales team to work together smoothly, share insights, and adapt collectively to changing market trends. The interplay between a positive culture and sales performance forms a powerful combination for sustained success and resilience in the fast-paced world of equipment dealership sales.

When considering customer relationships, the ideal scenario is when a customer starts treating your salesperson as a part of their own team. This kind of relationship fosters ongoing sales and profitability. Consider whether your salespeople genuinely enjoy visiting customer sites to collaborate on projects that benefit the customer. This isn't about instructing your salespeople to do so, but about them being genuinely enthusiastic in their interactions with customers. Salespeople who demonstrate this level of engagement are the ones who will be truly valued by customers.

Defining Sales Department Culture

Creating a vibrant and effective culture within an equipment dealership sales department is crucial. It's not just about meeting quotas or closing sales; it involves building a team driven by a common purpose and enthusiasm. Envision a culture where teamwork flourishes, where each member is a vital contributor to the dealership's success. This culture should encourage innovation and the free exchange of ideas, keeping the sales team responsive to customer needs and proactive in adapting to industry trends.

Recall the earlier discussion in this book about "Inspiring a Shared Vision." It's your role to create and passionately share this vision with your team, not just once a year, but perhaps at every sales meeting. Your sharing should be varied and relevant to keep the team engaged and excited.

A key element of a strong sales culture is a commitment to ongoing learning and development. Your team needs the skills and knowledge to navigate the complex field of industrial equipment sales. Cultivate a culture that values staying current with the latest technologies, market trends, and customer needs. Investing in continuous training ensures your sales department becomes a hub of expertise, providing unmatched value to clients in a constantly evolving industry.

Participation in professional organizations relevant to your industry is also beneficial. Some sales managers subscribe to services offering monthly book summaries, which can be a great source of new ideas for team education and motivation. Involvement in national or local sales groups can also provide access to innovative ideas from peers.

Effective communication is essential in any successful sales department culture. Encourage an environment where open and transparent communication is standard, fostering a team that operates cohesively and communicates seamlessly with clients, building lasting relationships and securing repeat business.

Regarding involvement with your sales team, regular interaction is key. Many sales managers I've seen have a schedule for accompanying salespeople on client visits and are also involved in major account calls. A structured approach to your weekly schedule, including sales meetings, time with salespeople, and time for administrative tasks, is crucial.

Finally, a sales department culture in an equipment dealership should balance results-driven focus with a human approach. Celebrate individual and team achievements, emphasizing customer satisfaction and long-term relationships. Success should be viewed not just in sales closed but in building a legacy of trust and excellence.

Recognition is a vital motivator for sales professionals. Creative approaches to acknowledging sales achievements, like the use of die-cast models or unique trophies, can significantly boost motivation and foster healthy competition within the team.

To enhance team dynamics, consider organizing quarterly meetings with distinct segments for training, strategic planning, recognition, and collaborative group projects. Creative initiatives like the use of symbolic trophies can cultivate a competitive spirit and encourage consistent performance.

Key Elements of a Positive Sales Culture a. Leadership

Leadership is the cornerstone in the intricate design of a sales department's culture, playing a critical role in shaping its character and substance. A visionary and influential leader not only sets the tone but also embodies the core values and principles central to the desired culture. By presenting a clear and inspiring vision, nurturing a sense of purpose, and leading by example, effective leaders create a sense of shared identity within the team. They direct the collective attitude, underscoring the significance of teamwork, creativity, and a focus on the customer. Through regular communication and a visible commitment to the cultural values, leaders become the architects of an environment where each team member is an essential participant in a shared mission. The impact of leadership on culture goes beyond words, extending into everyday actions and choices that reinforce the norms, thereby forging a unified and dynamic work environment.

At the heart of a strong sales department culture is the foundation of trust and transparency. Building trust is an ongoing process that leaders must continuously foster. Open communication about the organization's objectives, plans, and challenges creates an atmosphere of honesty and openness. When team members are kept in the loop and involved in decision-making, they become more engaged and offer their best efforts. Trust is further reinforced by leaders who exhibit consistent integrity, ensuring their actions match their words and maintaining high ethical standards. Transparency also means acknowledging both achievements and challenges, promoting a culture where learning from all experiences is valued. In an environment grounded in trust and transparency, individuals feel empowered to collaborate effectively, take thoughtful risks, and work together towards common goals, establishing a resilient and high-performing sales culture.

Communication

Open lines of communication form the lifeblood of a thriving sales department culture. Establishing a workplace where team members feel comfortable expressing their ideas, concerns, and insights is fundamental to fostering a dynamic and innovative environment. Leaders who actively encourage and facilitate open communication create a culture where information flows freely, breaking down silos and promoting a sense of collective ownership. Whether through regular team meetings, town halls, or digital communication platforms, providing avenues for dialogue ensures that everyone is on the same page, aligning their efforts with organizational goals. This openness enhances collaboration and empowers salespeople to share diverse perspectives, contributing to a richer and more adaptable sales culture.

Encouraging feedback and collaboration within a sales department is a catalyst for continuous improvement and heightened team performance. Leaders who actively seek input from team members demonstrate respect for individual contributions and create a culture that values learning and development. Whether formal or informal, feedback mechanisms serve as valuable tools for identifying areas of improvement, refining strategies, and recognizing outstanding performance. Collaboration is similarly crucial, as it fosters a collective mindset where the strengths of individual team members complement one another. By fostering an environment that celebrates collaboration and welcomes diverse viewpoints, leaders contribute to the creation of a resilient and adaptive sales culture that thrives on innovation and shared success.

Think about an idea. You have hired a new salesperson from a competitor, and they have been with you for four months. Maybe you could have them present different sales approaches they learned before joining you to your current team. Then, spend some time in a roundtable discussion with all your salespeople about how those sales styles will or will not work. Also, consider asking the team how they would handle that approach if the competition used it against them. The more you can involve this new salesperson in your team, the quicker they will be a solid team member, but they are also capable of bringing new ideas to your team.

Employee Recognition

Acknowledging and rewarding achievements should be a cornerstone of your approach. In the realm of equipment sales recognizing milestones and successes is pivotal. We understand that the journey in the industrial domain involves overcoming challenges, meeting targets, and driving innovation. By acknowledging these achievements, we not only celebrate the hard work and dedication of our salespeople but also inspire a culture of excellence.

Fostering a sense of value and accomplishment is deeply ingrained in our business philosophy. We believe that every accomplishment, whether big or small, contributes to the overall success of a business. In the world of North American industrial equipment, where precision and efficiency are paramount, cultivating a culture that values individual and collective achievements is crucial. You need to work hand in hand with your staff to create an environment where every team member feels valued and recognized for their unique contributions. This sense of accomplishment not only boosts morale but also drives continuous improvement, innovation, and a shared commitment to success.

Common Culture Pitfalls

In the landscape of equipment dealerships, effective communication is the linchpin of success, and your style places a strong emphasis on addressing any lack thereof. When communication breaks down, it creates a ripple effect that can undermine the entire operation. Dealerships face unique challenges that necessitate clear and constant communication. Without it, vital information can be lost in translation, leading to misunderstandings, missed opportunities, and a general sense of disconnection within the team.

The consequences of poor communication in the realm of sales management are profound. It can result in delayed responses to customer inquiries, misalignment in sales strategies, and a breakdown in customer relationships. In an industry where precision and reliability are paramount, any lapse in communication can lead to costly errors and a negative impact on the dealership's reputation. Moreover, internal cohesion suffers, leading to decreased morale and overall productivity among team members. Recognizing and mitigating these consequences is a key aspect of managing the sales force.

To counteract the challenges posed by a lack of communication, we advocate for strategic approaches to improve communication channels within the dealership. This involves fostering a culture of openness and transparency, where team members feel empowered to express their ideas and concerns. Implementing regular team meetings, utilizing communication technologies, and providing training on effective communication are integral strategies. Additionally, you as a manager need to encourage the establishment of clear protocols for information sharing, ensuring that crucial details about products, customer needs, and market trends are disseminated efficiently. By prioritizing and enhancing communication channels, sales managers can not only avert the negative consequences of poor communication but also foster a collaborative and thriving sales management environment.

Micromanagement

Micromanagement in equipment dealerships can have a detrimental impact on both morale and performance. Micromanaging erodes the trust between managers and sales representatives and stifles autonomy and creativity. Micromanagement undermines this empowerment, leading to a sense of frustration and disengagement among the team. When individuals feel trusted to make decisions and contribute their unique skills, morale soars, and performance improves. We encourage a leadership approach that values autonomy, fostering an environment where sales representatives are empowered to take ownership of their responsibilities, resulting in a more motivated and high-performing team.

High Turnover

High turnover is a pervasive challenge in dealerships, and you need to prioritize addressing the signs of discontent to foster a workplace culture that retains top talent. Recognizing indicators such as declining performance, increased absenteeism, or a lack of enthusiasm is crucial for proactive management. Understanding the unique needs and aspirations of each sales team member is key. We advocate for personalized engagement strategies, including regular check-ins, career development discussions, and creating a positive work environment that values contributions. By actively listening to concerns, addressing issues promptly, and providing opportunities for growth, you can instill a sense of loyalty and job satisfaction, mitigating the factors contributing to high turnover and ultimately retaining top talent in the competitive landscape of equipment dealerships.

Resistance to Change

Resistance to change is a common challenge faced by managers. We approach this obstacle with a combination of empathy and strategic communication. When introducing changes in processes, technology, or sales strategies within the sales department it's essential to recognize that resistance often stems from fear of the unknown or a perceived threat to job security. You should address resistance within the team by fostering an open dialogue. Managers should actively listen to concerns, provide context for the changes, and involve team members in decision-making when possible. This inclusive approach helps build a sense of ownership and shared commitment to the success of the implemented changes.

Typically, resistance to change stems from the disruption it poses to the established routines of salespeople. It's not that they inherently dislike the new concept; they are hesitant to relinquish their sense of control. The daily patterns they've adhered to for an extended period become ingrained in their work habits. To successfully implement change, it is crucial not only to introduce the new idea but also to monitor and emphasize its importance actively. Salespeople may dismiss the new activity without consistent attention and reinforcement and revert to their familiar, old routines.

Effectively communicating the benefits of change should be a key pillar of your methodology. Managers must articulate how the proposed changes align with the team's overall goals, enhance efficiency, and contribute to individual and collective success. Whether it involves adopting new technologies, refining sales processes, or embracing innovative approaches, highlighting the positive impact on job satisfaction, career development, and overall performance is crucial. We encourage managers to present change as an opportunity for growth and improvement, linking it to the team's success and fostering a mindset that embraces adaptation as a catalyst for long-term success in the competitive landscape of equipment dealerships.

12. Building Professional Salespeople

Career Path Development & Gross Profit Expectations

Sales Skills Development	Account Maturity		
	Low	Medium	High
High	$240,000	$300,000	$360,000
Medium	$180,000	$240,000	$300,000
Low	$120,000	$180,000	$240,000

To attract and retain quality salespeople, you must be able to provide a clear career path for their growth. They must be able to see ways they can grow in professional development, job responsibility and income.

As you know, the target gross profit per commercial salesperson is $240,000 per year. Not all salespeople, especially new ones-will reach this level of gross profit. On the other hand, top salespeople calling on mature accounts may achieve more than $240,000 in gross profit annually.

As you assign accounts to salespeople, you will naturally want to assign high maturity accounts to your most skilled salespeople. You will assign low maturity accounts to your rookie salespeople. This allows you to establish a grid that shows a clear career path to your salespeople.

Sales Skills Development	Account Maturity		
	Low	Medium	High
High	$240,000	$300,000	$360,000
Medium	$180,000	$240,000	$300,000
Low	$120,000	$180,000	$240,000

The numbers in the grid refer to annual sales gross profit by salesperson. In the example, a rookie salesperson assigned to only low maturity accounts has been given a goal (or quota) of $120,000 in annual gross profit. On the other extreme, a highly skilled veteran salesperson assigned mature accounts has been given a goal of $360,000. Other salespeople with various skills have been assigned to accounts with various levels of maturity. Look at the table to see how they have been assigned.

Sales Skills Development	Account Maturity		
	Low	**Medium**	**High**
High	$240,000	$300,000	$360,000
Medium	$180,000	$240,000	$300,000
Low	$120,000	$180,000	$240,000

You can build your own grid for your company, putting in whatever gross profit figures you want. However, for the sake of example, let's assume the figures in the grid apply to your company.

Sales Skills Development	Account Maturity		
	Low	**Medium**	**High**
High	$240,000	$300,000	$360,000
Medium	$180,000	$240,000	$300,000
Low	$120,000	$180,000	$240,000

Imagine you are hiring a new salesperson. You can show the salesperson the grid, explain your expectations of salespeople and simultaneously show him or her an attractive career path.

Show the goal for the first year.

Explain where you expect the salesperson to be at the end of the first year by drawing a star in the bottom left hand box as shown.

Sales training process and goals for the second year.

Explain your training program and how the salesperson will develop skills and begin to penetrate accounts. As he or she does that, the accounts will become more mature. Draw the second star and label it "2." By the end of the second year, you expect the salesperson to be at the second star.

The importance of ongoing improvement and third year goals.

Explain how the salesperson will continue to develop skills and continue to penetrate accounts. Draw a star showing your expectations for the third year and label it "3."

Show continued growth expectations.

Continue to explain how the salesperson will grow and your expectations for year 4.

Explain your expectations for year 5.

By following this process, you can show salespeople a career path. Having shared your expectations with them, you can help them develop their own personal training plan to help them acquire the skills and abilities to make it all happen.

Learning Curve

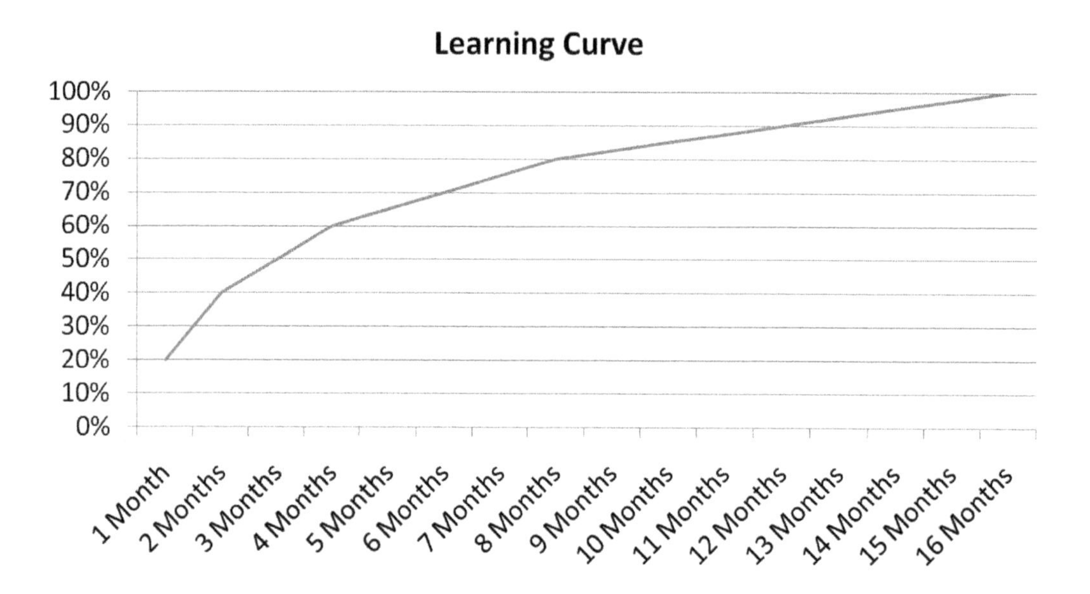

Areas of Training

Stop and think for a minute about everything a salesperson must know or be able to do to sell successfully in today's complex market. Competition is tougher than ever before. Customers are more knowledgeable about alternatives. Their expectations are higher. They are less willing than ever before to put up with poor quality or poor service. Their accounting systems are sophisticated enough to provide them with irrefutable data about their tire purchases and long-term tire experiences. Most fleets have quality control initiatives in place that provide information about and analysis of problems, whereas in the past, few even recognized, much less categorized or attempted to solve, these problems.

Yes, it's a tough and difficult market out there. Your salespeople must not only survive in this market, they must manage their resources to succeed. Your company's success depends on your salespeople's ability to build long-term relationships with customers who are more professional and knowledgeable than at any time in history.

In this environment, knowledge becomes the most important competitive weapon for your salespeople. It is your responsibility to help them obtain that knowledge.

These four types of knowledge are critical to the success of your salespeople:

- Product knowledge
- Company knowledge
- Customer knowledge
- Selling strategy knowledge

Product Knowledge

"Product knowledge" refers to more than your salespeople's knowledge of the equipment you sell. In addition to knowing the products you sell, your salespeople must be able to apply that knowledge to help customers solve their application problems. They must also be able to demonstrate the differences and advantages of the product your company recommends and prove that these differences and advantages are compelling enough to cause the prospect to buy.

Therefore, your salespeople must know

- how and where to apply their products.
- advantages and disadvantages of competitive products.
- warranty information.
- information about company & manufacturer programs.
- information about sales tools.
- your company's pricing strategies

Company Knowledge

In addition to having a thorough understanding of product and product-related information, your salespeople must also know and be able to present information about your company and about the brand or manufacturer.

Research among customers in various industries clearly shows that trust is the most important factor affecting customers' buying decisions. If a salesperson and his/her company are not credible and trustworthy, a prospect will not buy.

Customer Knowledge

"Customer knowledge" refers to both knowledge of the market area and knowledge of individual customers and their needs.

Market area knowledge is a big picture view of changes and trends occurring in the transportation industry. Salespeople must stay current on the rapid and continuous changes in equipment, transportation, vehicles, tires and other products.

For example, if a trend is developing in the industry toward higher-fuel-economy vehicles, the salesperson must be aware of that trend and maximize selling opportunities by presenting tire solutions that maximize fuel economy. Ignoring such a trend can have devastating effects on a salesperson's productivity.

Individual customer knowledge refers to an understanding of a fleet's problems, needs and opportunities. Although fleets are affected by market trends, each fleet has its unique needs. The only way for a salesperson to really understand a fleet's individual needs is through data collection activities such as fleet inspection and scrap tire analysis.

Selling Strategy Knowledge

All the knowledge in the world is useless until a salesperson uses that knowledge to sell programs, services, information and products to prospects. The goal of every sales activity must be to build a long-term, mutually profitable relationship. Ideally, this relationship must be so successful that the salesperson's company becomes the sole supplier to the customer.

Knowledge of selling strategy includes knowing about and using:

- the Selling Process.
- the buying process.
- sales skills such as questioning, listening, objection handling and closing.
- negotiation skills

Product

Most manufacturers do a very credible job explaining, teaching and training salespeople and other company staff on their products, features and sometimes the benefits. Our recommendation is to always use that as your first level of training. You might have unique local needs or niche positions for some categories of your manufacturer's products and these might need to be trained specifically by you as the sales manager.

Sales Process

We'll talk at more length about the sales process later, but salespeople that have not had some formal sales training frequently benefit by just knowing the basic points of the sales process. With these they can determine where in the sales cycle they are with a particular prospect or customer. Basic categories of the sales process are in the diagram below.

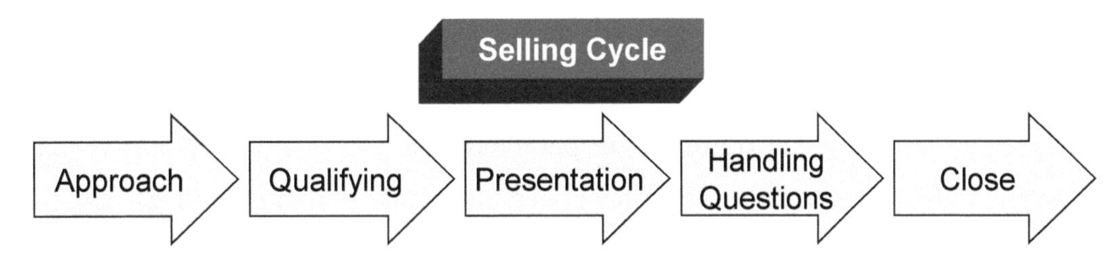

Computers

While today many of the new employees entering the job market are experiencing carpal tunnel syndrome from playing video games so much, not all are completely trained in the use of computers for doing letters, emails, quotations, and call tracking. It might either need to be a job skill that you require before hiring or a skill that you chose to train. Sometimes this will depend on the talent of the applicant in other areas.

Handling Objections

Many salespeople shy away from cold calls because of the anticipated volume of rejection and also avoid anything in a sales process that would create tension, confrontation or require negotiations. These salespeople are avoiding conflict in the belief that it creates friction and erodes the "close relationship" they have been trying to build.

As sales manager you should be teaching salespeople how to plan for objections, how to lay the groundwork for creating objections that the salesperson already have the skills to counter. If prospects and customers do not raise objections sometimes the salesperson should bring up what they might be thinking and explain why that frequent objection by many other people is not valid with this product or your company.

Objections indicate that the potential customer is thinking through the entire purchase or process. It demonstrates areas that they feel are valid, and it allows the salesperson to validate the value they are bringing to the purchase.

There are entire books written on handling objections. This book merely has time to mention the importance of it, and tell you that your job is to teach the salespeople why it is critical to learn how to anticipate and then to handle objections.

Customer Satisfaction

Customer satisfaction is sometimes discussed as what we wish to achieve and something to be measured. Here in talking about training salespeople we want to focus on teaching what drives most customers to feel or report that they have been taken care of and are at least satisfied.

When you ask customers in many different industries and professions what they value most, and what makes them feel that the salesperson has really gone out of their way to take care of them we find a number of comments high on the list:

- Good communications
- Regular and quick response
- Integrity about the company, product service and delivery

Many years ago, the First Bank of Chicago asked for research and survey of their customers about what was important to them in achieving customer satisfaction. One of the most interesting points to this list is how universal it is.

10 Most Important Service Attributes

- Being called when promised.
- Receiving an explanation of how a problem happened.
- Providing customers with information so they know
    - the number(s) to call
    - methods to keep apprized of equipment status
- Being contacted promptly when a problem is resolved.
- Being allowed to talk to someone in authority.
- Being told how long it will take to resolve a problem.
- Being given useful alternatives if a problem can't be resolved.
- Treating customers like people, not account numbers.
- Being told about ways to help prevent problems in the future.
- Being given progress reports if a problem cannot be resolved immediately.

As Identified By Customers

"Marketing Services: Competing Through Quality" Leonard Bery & A. Parasuraman
from Research by First National Bank of Chicago

Scripts for Salespeople

When trying to support and train employees one of the methods is to lead by example. Some employees are afraid of confrontation and by supplying them with a script of how to handle the question, issue or phone call you provide them not only the example that you might show them in person, but a written script of what to say. They need to learn that this is not to be "verbatim" every time, but should be a strong direction of how to respond to some objections, questions or issues that come their way.

This "script approach" works well for young or inexperienced salespeople, but can also be used for other employees in the company when you are changing or implementing new procedures. By writing out the "script" of what should be said in many cases you take away the fear of confrontation and what they should say when a prospect or customer calls or talks to them about new company policies. This provides them support and confidence in answering. That confidence will then come across to the customer as common agreement within the company about what the person is talking about.

Learning Styles

As the sales manager you job is to "get results." Whether you do it by yelling or sending memos, talking quietly or posting billboards is not the question, just get the results! Of course sometimes your methods might impact the outcome, so those could have an impact on whether you accomplish the results. So what about someone who is very detailed as a new employee?

Some employees will learn the product, the sales job or other features of their job from books, some from lectures, some from going out and succeeding or failing. Each person has their own learning style. Your job is not to shape them all to learn a certain way, but to find what works best for them and to organize a way for that to happen that is successful for them and you. How do they get results? Find it and make it happen.

In one company, there were two salespeople; one made many calls and defined the relationship and needs until he knew that the next step was to be there in person, the other salesperson scheduled many in-person visits with prospects. The results were they were both closing the same amount of business. Other than their expense variance, who's selling style was better? They both had different styles that were successful. This is the type of different style issue you need to look at in learning and figure out what works with each salesperson you are responsible for directing.

Strategic Planning by & for Accounts

When you have your weekly or monthly meeting with your salesperson, you are reviewing what has happened, but you should also be planning what is coming. One of the critical planning sessions is to plan the strategic direction of each account with the salesperson.

Look at the section later in the book for organizing your review and planning sessions with the salesperson for how to organize your schedule and agenda for this type of meeting.

Looking at an account you want train the salesperson to look at the large picture and then organize the details to accomplish it. So you would begin looking at the prospect company, their purchasing approach, their requirements, the annual purchasing budget or allocations and number of equipment units they have or need. Then you look at the current situation, the relationship the salesperson has with the representatives of the company, how many different people are involved in purchasing decisions, etc. From these elements you begin to layout the "goal" of working with the company, "the solution you can provide." Then you look at the current position you are in, and where it needs improvement.

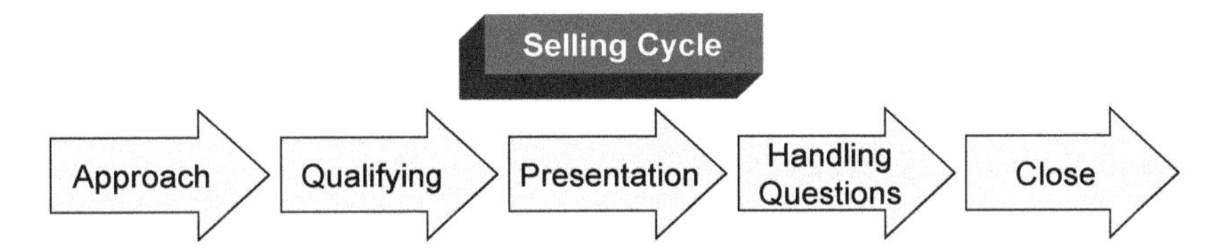

Remembering five steps of the selling cycle you might determine that some additional work needs to be done in the "Qualifying" step, before you proceed to the "Presentation." It helps to look at the Selling Cycle while planning the strategy regarding the account. You might want to put a timeline on the cycle also. When is the prospect interested in having the product delivered, close the deal or have their presentation? Knowing some of these answers will help in developing the strategy for this account. Also going back to the "Evolution of The Market" will help in determining the purchasing philosophy of the prospect.

Many things have to be taken into account in teaching a salesperson how to organize the strategy regarding an account. The salesperson might need to assess the purchasing philosophy as we were discussing, or they may need to be working on a solution for the prospect that is unique from their competition.

The point here is not to always deliver the Strategic Plan for the salesperson, but to teach them how to create a Strategic Plan for their accounts.

Developing Salespeople's Careers

Depending on your company, what branches you have, the products you represent and the openness to promotion that your company has will determine the upward options that you can offer. Many salespeople will succeed in sales volume increases, better gross profits on those accounts they cover and better penetration of their accounts.

Some salespeople are good at sales but they also yearn for responsibility and recognition. Sometimes this will be accomplished by their incremental sales changes, but for others it needs to be a role in sales management or branch management. As the sales manager you need to be assessing your salespeople to determine where they will contribute to the company and what the company needs that they can provide.

This might be a simple as asking salespeople what they want to do in five years, or you might use sales and management assessment tools or tests.

Building a Positive Sales Culture

Training and Development

In dealerships, prioritizing training and development is central to our philosophy. Recognizing the dynamic nature of industrial equipment sales, your approach to training will underscore the significance of ongoing training programs. These programs serve as a cornerstone for keeping the sales team abreast of industry trends, technological advancements, and evolving customer needs. By investing in continuous learning, managers can ensure that their team remains agile and well-equipped to navigate the complexities of the ever-changing market.

Wise Wolf Consulting places a strong emphasis on professional growth of the team as an investment in the dealership's success. Beyond initial onboarding, providing avenues for ongoing professional development fosters a culture of excellence and commitment. This involves technical training and soft skills enhancement, such as effective communication and customer relationship management. Identify individual strengths and areas for improvement within your team, tailoring training initiatives to cultivate a well-rounded skill set. Review Chapter 10 on Recruiting and Training regarding this area. By investing in the holistic development of their sales team, managers can position the dealership for sustained growth and success in the competitive landscape of industrial equipment sales.

Furthermore, we advocate for a proactive approach to training and development, aligning programs with the dealership's strategic goals. This ensures that the team is not only proficient in current practices but also poised to adapt to future challenges. Remember the four Phases of the Market we discussed in chapter one about the Evolving Market. Investing in the professional growth of the team goes beyond a one-time effort; it's an ongoing commitment to staying ahead in the industry. Foster a learning culture that encourages collaboration, knowledge sharing, and a mindset of continuous improvement. In doing so, you not only elevate the skills of individual team members but also cultivate a collective expertise that propels the dealership to new heights in the competitive market.

We expect you will have a three-pronged approach to training. You are the primary one to design or deliver the department training. This could include sales techniques, product features or how to handle objections. Securing regular outside training demonstrates to your team the importance you place on their development; semi-annual or annual training events are one way to not lose track of this. Then encourage or require each salesperson to get involved in their own level of training. This could be as simple as belonging to a Toastmaster's group or completing an online course regularly.

Team-building Activities

Team-building activities play a pivotal role in fostering a sense of camaraderie and encouraging teamwork—this should be a cornerstone of your philosophy. A traditional example that has proven effective is organizing team-building retreats. These retreats offer a change of environment, allowing team members to interact in a more relaxed setting. Through activities such as trust falls, problem-solving challenges, and collaborative exercises, individuals bond, creating a foundation of trust and camaraderie that transcends the workplace. Such traditional activities provide a space for team members to connect on a personal level, enhancing their ability to work seamlessly together in the professional arena. Sometimes it can be as simple as the team going bowling.

For a more challenging team-building experience, consider outdoor adventure activities like a ropes course or a wilderness survival expedition. These activities demand trust, communication, and collaboration in high-pressure situations, pushing team members out of their comfort zones. Overcoming physical challenges in a team setting fosters resilience, reinforces the importance of collective effort, and builds a shared sense of accomplishment. While demanding, these experiences can strengthen bonds and instill a sense of unity that transcends the daily challenges of industrial equipment sales.

Drawing inspiration from another industry, an unconventional team-building activity could involve a cooking class. The coordination required in a kitchen setting mirrors the need for synchronized efforts in the dealership. As team members collaborate to create a meal, they learn to communicate effectively, delegate tasks, and adapt to unforeseen challenges—skills directly transferable to the world of equipment sales. This non-traditional approach injects an element of novelty into team building, fostering a creative and collaborative spirit that can positively impact the dealership's overall cohesion and performance.

Inclusive Environment

Within the dealership realm, fostering an inclusive environment is a fundamental tenet emphasizing the importance of diversity and inclusion. This goes beyond mere acknowledgment of differences; it involves actively seeking and valuing the unique perspectives, backgrounds, and experiences each team member brings. By celebrating diversity, managers can harness a wealth of creativity and innovation, enhancing the dealership's adaptability in the dynamic market. Don't forget that your customers are not a homogenous group of people. Your staff needs to be comfortable interacting with the diverse environment they will encounter in sales calls.

Embracing diversity and inclusion is not just a box to check; it's a commitment to creating an environment where every team member feels valued. We advocate for policies and practices that ensure equal opportunities for professional growth and recognition. This involves addressing unconscious biases, providing training on cultural competence, and actively promoting an atmosphere of respect. An inclusive environment ensures that every voice is heard and every contribution is acknowledged, creating a sense of belonging that fuels individual and collective success.

To truly ensure everyone feels valued, we encourage managers to go beyond superficial gestures. It involves actively soliciting feedback, listening to concerns, and addressing any disparities in recognition or opportunities. Managers play a crucial role in fostering an inclusive culture where differences are not just accepted but embraced. When team members feel seen, heard, and valued for their unique contributions, it enhances morale and cultivates a collaborative spirit that propels the dealership to new heights in the competitive market.

In summary, your approach needs to be an inclusive one.

Measuring and Monitoring Culture

Measuring and monitoring the sales culture is paramount for success. Managers must establish metrics that go beyond traditional performance indicators to holistically evaluate the sales culture's health. This involves considering factors such as employee satisfaction, collaboration, and adherence to the dealership's core values. By developing comprehensive metrics, managers gain insights into the intangible elements that contribute to a positive and productive workplace culture within the sales environment.

Regular check-ins and feedback loops are integral components of the management approach to maintaining a healthy sales culture. Managers are encouraged to conduct frequent assessments, engaging in open and honest conversations with team members to gauge their experiences and perceptions. These check-ins serve as valuable feedback loops, allowing managers to identify potential issues, address concerns, and celebrate successes in real time. By staying attuned to the pulse of the sales team, managers can proactively nurture a culture that fosters collaboration, innovation, and a shared commitment to the dealership's mission.

That last paragraph was a longwinded way of saying you need call reports, quote logs, close rates and market share for each salesperson, but you also need to look at their attitude, their connection to customers and prospects, their motivation and intensity to get a fully rounded picture of each of your staff.

To effectively measure the success of the sales culture, it's important to utilize both quantitative and qualitative data. Beyond sales figures, managers should leverage employee surveys, focus groups, and performance reviews to gather diverse perspectives. By combining numerical data with qualitative insights, managers gain a more nuanced understanding of the intricacies of the sales culture, enabling them to make informed decisions and implement targeted interventions as needed. This commitment to continuous improvement ensures that the sales culture evolves in sync with the ever-changing demands of the industrial equipment sales landscape.

Managing Salespeople & The Department

Structuring the Sales Department

There are three basic tools for helping your salespeople maximize their success with accounts:

- Sales Call Frequency And History
- Call Scheduling
- Quote Log

Sales Call Frequency And History

Tracking sales call frequency and history is essential to helping salespeople plan their time to achieve maximum results. To track sales call frequency and history, you must be able to sort data by

- salesperson name.
- account ID.
- account category (Existing, Conquest, Prospect, Suspect).
- contact frequency (dates of calls).
- contact history (what happened on each call).

Sales Call Tracking Methodology

To track sales call frequency and history, you and your salespeople must have a methodology of recording information about fleets and what happened on sales calls to those fleets.

Today, most companies have electronically automated sales call tracking or are considering automating it. There are hundreds of "contact management" software applications available. The best known are SalesForce™, Act™ and Goldmine™.

Whether your company uses an electronic tracking system or a manual paper system, the information you need and the ways to access it are similar.

Suppose you decide to use a manual system and you hire a new salesperson. Tell the salesperson to go to the local stationary store to buy 200 file folders and a milk crate. Have the salesperson put each of his/her target accounts' names on a tab on each file folder. Put the basic information about the account from the Account Profile inside the folder.

Have the salesperson divide all target accounts by category using colored metal clips on the file folders. Existing Accounts folders get a red clip, Conquest Accounts folders get a blue clip and Prospect Accounts folders get a yellow clip.

Have your salespeople complete call reports and send one copy to you and place the other copy in the folder for that fleet.

Establishing this system helps you direct the activities of your salespeople. When you ask a salesperson to review their Existing Accounts with you, they simply pull all the red clipped folders. Those folders will include all the information about those accounts: basic fleet data, dates of sales calls and what happened on each call.

Simultaneously, you should keep your own folders for each of your company's Existing Accounts and Conquest Accounts. (You may also want to track sales calls on Prospect Accounts and Suspect Accounts.) Using the data in those folders, you can build your own report of sales call frequency and history. You can then analyze your salespeople's coverage of the market. You can analyze how many calls they are making in each category, how many times they are calling on each fleet, and you can organize this information according to salesperson for easy reference.

If you are using a manual tracking system a Sales Call Frequency And History Report is available for use in the Tools section of this module.

By comparing actual dollar sales reports from your accounting department with the data on your call frequency form, you can analyze sales volume per call to determine whether your people are spending their time optimally. By looking at call frequency and history, you can see how your salespeople are leading customers through the Selling Process and you can analyze cycle time. You can spot areas where salespeople seem to have trouble advancing the sale.

The manual contact management system described above requires manual sorting of information and duplicate entry of data on separate forms, manual analysis of that data and shuffling of numerous papers to make sense of it and draw conclusions. Those are just a few of the reasons an electronic contact management system is so attractive. You can set up your contact management application to work in the same fashion as the manual system, except that the application itself serves as virtual folders and milk crates. Instead of sending you a copy of each call report, your salespeople will simply download their data to your computer regularly. You can then sort and analyze the data quickly with minimal data entry and no duplication of entry or paperwork.

Whether you create, sort and analyze data manually or electronically is not the critical element. What is important is that you have your salespeople keep accurate records of their activities and send copies to you. You cannot maximize your return on your investment in salespeople unless you direct those salespeople to spend their time and expertise in the right ways; that means doing the right things with the right accounts at the right time.

This methodology of managing accounts is not new or revolutionary. It is something that top salespeople have done forever. Top salespeople know that success is not about geographic territory management or about the latest objection-handling technique or the deal of the day. Instead, sales success is about salespeople prioritizing accounts and managing their activities with the high priority accounts.

This methodology simply organizes what top salespeople have always known into a system you can and must implement throughout your entire sales force.

Sales Call Scheduling

Sales call scheduling is a matter of salespeople calling on the right fleets and utilizing their time effectively.

Because you've figured your sales capacity, you know how many calls you have available. Because you analyzed size, priority and category, you have selected target accounts that offer you high potential sales and profitability. Because you've developed a list of target accounts, you know who should be called on most because you know the fleets that will drive your market share.

There are two parts of managing sales call scheduling:

- Make sure your salespeople call on the target accounts.
- Help your salespeople maximize their face-to-face selling time with the right accounts.

That requires your salespeople to manage their time within the geography in which they work.

Sales success is not about geographical territory management but about account management. Nevertheless, you must help your salespeople maximize their selling time within their geographic area.

Helping your salespeople organize their schedules and work in an organized fashion minimizes windshield time. If you don't help them organize their time proactively, they will bounce from one account to another in a reactive fashion. That only wastes valuable selling time.

You must help your salespeople organize a time management plan and you must insist they work in accordance with the plan.

Organizing a time management plan for salespeople is similar to your company's production manager organizing the retread shop. Craftsmen in your retread shop don't arrive at work and decide what to do every day. They know in advance because your production operation is organized. Yet, without your help, your salespeople may tend to begin each day wondering what they will do today, who they should call on and what routes of travel they should take.

To achieve maximum success, your sales department should be just as well-structured and as well-organized as a well-managed team.

Organizing time management plans for salespeople begins with· identifying the accounts assigned to each salesperson. Because sales success is based on account management and because you must assign your best salespeople to the accounts with the largest potential, your account assignment will be based on accounts and salesperson expertise, not on geographical territories.

Have each salesperson mark his/her assigned accounts on a map of your market area. Have them put colored dots or push-pins on the map to mark their target accounts as follows: Existing Accounts-red, Conquest Accounts-blue, Prospect Accounts-yellow.

Refer to the number of calls you expect your salespeople to make annually on each account. Divide those numbers by 50 to determine the calls per week for each account.

Look at the map the salesperson has prepared. Work with the salesperson to establish routes of travel and call frequency to make the required number of calls on each account in each account category.

You will see that fate did not conveniently place all the target Existing Accounts right next to each other. Chances are, they are scattered all over your market area. Likewise, target Conquest Accounts are probably not conveniently grouped.

You must help each of your salespeople establish call patterns that minimize windshield time and maximize face-to-face selling time with the accounts that offer the most potential. You must help your salespeople plan and work in blocks of time and in an organized fashion. Whether you manage call frequency and call history manually or electronically, you must use a map for call scheduling.

Quote Log

As your salespeople make their sales calls, they will be preparing and presenting proposals to their target accounts. Some of those proposals will be accepted and the account will become a customer or (in the case of Existing Accounts) will do more business with your company. Some proposals will fall on deaf ears and the fleet will continue to do what they've done in the past. Some proposals will be considered, but the fleet will purchase a package from a competitor.

You should review proposals with salespeople before they present them and you should provide input to those proposals. You should also keep a log of all quotations. Maintaining a log of proposals and quotations is essential to reviewing sales success with your salespeople and to helping direct their activities. Your quote log also provides the data to help you calculate participation and closure rates.

Your quote log should include the following information:

- Quote number
- Date
- Salesperson name
- Customer name and ID
- Tire models
- Number of units
- Price quoted
- Type of deal
- Gross Profit
- Miscellaneous notes

- Status of quote
  - Working
  - Abandoned
  - Lost
  - Sold
  - Budget
  - Re-quote
  - Optional
- Change of status date
- If sold, reasons for sale
- If lost, competitor lost to, price lost at, and reason for loss

The Professional Sales Impression

Grooming & Dress

You might have company shirts, jackets or full uniforms. Just be clear about what your expectations of dress and grooming are for salespeople and other staff and then be consistent about your follow through. If you have a casual day of the week, then define what you mean by casual in your company, geography and industry. What is casual for one southern dealership might be ridiculous and cause customer avoidance in a northern dealership.

Printed, Email and Communications

Visual presentation is subtle but establishes your quality. A well organized and formatted presentation for quotations, invoices and customer needs analysis tell the customer about the salesperson's qualities. Be sure your sales staff is checking spelling, grammar and general organization of their materials. Today's technology should make this simpler.

Your staff, as well as your company should have standardized Email Signatures, and standardized styles and format for their emails.

When salespeople or staff answer land lines or mobile phones they should be professional in their style. “Yeah!” is not an acceptable opening statement. But you don’t want them so formal that the customer feels put off by their response. Think about how your staff handles phones, and there are companies out there that will come to you and train everyone on how to handle communications.

Accessories & Transportation

Don’t think your customers and prospects don’t notice you company cars, trucks, employee vehicles, computers, smartphones, etc. Clean vehicles, that don’t break down is also a reflection on your service, even if you don’t service your own cars and trucks. While you may not have the leading edge in cpmputer or smartphones you need quality ones that accomplish their function without probelsm.

13. The Sales Manager as Coach

When some managers think of sales training, they think of selling skills: techniques such as questioning, listening, objection handling and closing. While those skills may be important, they alone won't provide sales success. Sales managers must also provide other, ongoing training about markets, products, competitors, information gathering processes and a myriad of other subjects.

It is said that we live in the Information Age. Information and knowing what to do with it is a competitive weapon; a weapon that can lead your salespeople - and, therefore, your company-to greater success.

Regardless of how much your salespeople know, they need coaching to help them compete at top effectiveness. Coaching is a crucial task for sales managers.

Coaching is a process that provides the opportunity for continuous improvement of your salespeople.

The Coaching Process

Coaching is an essential part of achieving long-term results as you build a great sales team. As their coach, you will help your salespeople fine tune their application of the selling process. Your overall success as a manager depends on your coaching ability. Just implementing "training" will not maintain the skills you want your salepeople to have. There is a process called "The Forgetting Curve."

The forgetting curve, a concept initially proposed by psychologist Hermann Ebbinghaus, is particularly relevant in the context of sales training. It illustrates how information is lost over time when there's no attempt to retain it. In sales, this phenomenon can significantly impact the effectiveness of training programs. For instance, after a comprehensive training session, a salesperson may initially remember the strategies, techniques, and information presented.

However, as per the forgetting curve, if these concepts aren't regularly revisited or applied, the retention rate rapidly declines. This means that without reinforcement (coaching), much of the training investment is at risk of being wasted as the knowledge fades from memory.

To combat the forgetting curve in sales training, continuous learning and regular reinforcement are crucial. This can be achieved through methods like spaced repetition, where key concepts are reviewed at increasing intervals, and practical application, where salespeople apply what they've learned in real-world scenarios. (That was a fancy sentence that I think describes weekly sales meetings.)

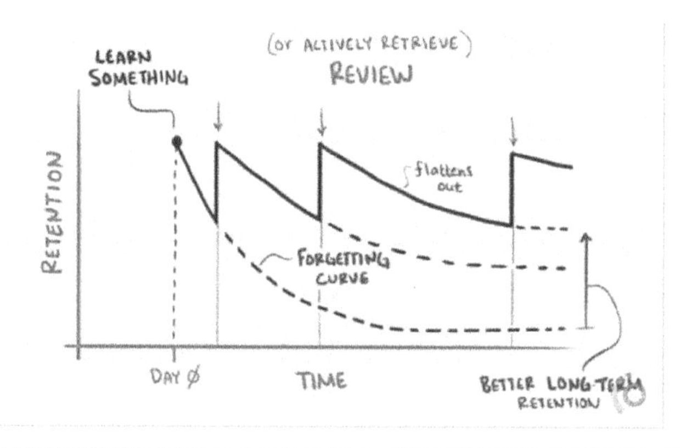

Figure 2 Each of the points is a function of some reinforcement of the original training process.

Additionally, using interactive training methods such as role-playing, simulations, and collaborative workshops can help in solidifying the knowledge. Sales managers can also encourage their teams to regularly discuss and share insights from their experiences, further reinforcing learning. By understanding that memory diminishes over time, sales training can be structured in a way that maximizes retention and ongoing proficiency.

Moreover, technology plays a significant role in mitigating the effects of the forgetting curve in sales training. Digital tools like Learning Management Systems (LMS) can be programmed to provide periodic refreshers and assessments, ensuring that the knowledge remains current in the sales team's mind. Mobile learning apps can offer bite-sized learning modules, quizzes, and flashcards for on-the-go revision, making it easier for sales professionals to keep their skills sharp. In the age of data analytics, tracking learning patterns and identifying areas where individuals are struggling can lead to more personalized and effective training approaches.

By leveraging technology, sales organizations can ensure a more enduring impact of their training programs, aligning with the natural patterns of memory retention and forgetting.

Today with the internet, apps and many other sources there are a extensive range of options for reinforcement and coaching support for sales training. One of the sales managers I worked with used to send his salespeople material from a publication called "TheSellingAdvantage.com." I'm only using this as an illustration of how he reinforced his training for his salespeople. He then would ask them in following sales meetings what they learned from that publication. This was a consistent coaching process for him and them.

While the decline in selling skills after 30 days was disappointing, the authors of Managing Major Sales did find some salespeople who actually gained skills during the same time period. The key difference in these individuals was the coaching they received during the post-training period.

Sales training alone won't produce the results you desire. Coaching makes the difference between excellent performance and mediocre performance.

Regardless of how talented your people are, they will have a tendency to become wrapped up in activities and not plan for maximum productivity. Since your job is to maximize their productivity, you want to help them focus on productivity first and then determine the priority of activities that will help them achieve that productivity.

What Is Coaching?

Coaching is a process of helping your salespeople improve their performance. Great coaches motivate, teach and reinforce learning. They help their salespeople develop their own abilities to the fullest, allowing them to contribute the maximum amount to the success of the business.

Coaching is different from disciplining or criticizing, both of which can be seen as negative and de-motivating. When you discipline or criticize, you are attempting to stop an undesired behavior. When you coach, you are working with a salesperson to improve performance.

To be an outstanding coach, you must coach your people to adhere to the selling process. As a coach, it isn't necessary that you be as talented as your salespeople.

They may have skills beyond your own. Your job is not to be better than they are, but to help them become better than they are.

Coaching is an ongoing, interactive process between the manager and the salesperson.

Coaching Principles

Coaching is a tool to help your salespeople and your company achieve greater results. There are five basic principles to using the tool most effectively.

- Coaching must maintain salesperson self-esteem.
- Coach according to the selling process.
- Coaching must be a collaborative effort between salesperson and manager.
- Objectives and action steps must be specific and measurable.
- Coaching must be continuous.

Coach To The Selling Process

You must coach your people to a follow a process. That means you will be asking questions such as, "Where is the prospect in his/her buying process?" and, "Where are you in the Selling Process?"

The steps to take in the selling process are totally dependent on where the prospect is in his/her buying process. Coaching helps salespeople focus on the activities that will yield the most productivity.

Collaborative Effort

If you or your salespeople view coaching as a dictatorial activity, your coaching efforts will fail. Your salespeople must view coaching as a process that can help them be more successful. They should view coaching as a collaborative effort they find motivating and useful.

During coaching sessions, you should listen actively to your salesperson's thoughts and suggestions. This builds confidence in the process of coaching and motivates salespeople to produce higher results. When salespeople reject coaching, it is often because they do not see it as a collaborative effort or because they don't think you care about their ideas or opinions.

Most salespeople appreciate having their manager ride with them and make sales calls with them. If your salespeople don't, there is probably something wrong with your personal coaching style. Until you figure out what is wrong and correct it, you will never be an effective coach.

Specific And Measurable

You and your salespeople should reach agreement on specific action steps that will yield the results you both desire.

Those action steps must be specific and measurable, allowing you and your salesperson to analyze what is working and what isn't. That means you can both learn from your experiences and share your learning with other salespeople on your sales team so everyone becomes more successful.

Continuous

Coaching is not an activity or an event. It is a process. That means it doesn't stop and start, but is ongoing.

You must coach your people every time you see them. It is only through continuous coaching that maximum results are achieved.

When you ride with your salespeople and make calls with them, you are setting aside time for coaching. That's important, but equally important is the time you take to coach your people when you see them casually.

Your goal throughout the coaching process is to create a competitive advantage for your selling team. You do that by identifying exactly how each individual can better use his/her skills and talents, then helping them do so.

Coaching On Sales Calls

As you have learned, you must continually look for opportunities to coach your people to higher levels of achievement. However, special considerations are important when you ride with your salespeople and make sales calls with them.

You will analyze the coaching steps in the following areas:

1. Before the sales call
2. During the sales call
3. After the sales call

Before The Sales Call

Before making a coaching sales call, do the following with your salesperson:

- Introduce coaching.
- Select the fleet.
- Determine the objective of the call.
- Discuss appropriate strategies.
- Discuss and clarify your role during the call.

Introduce Coaching

Introduce your sales team to the concept of coaching. Explain that you will work with them individually, observing sales calls, evaluating their strengths and areas for improvement.

It is a natural tendency for anyone to feel "intimidated" when the boss is watching. It is important to stress that you are there simply to observe; that your role is to help focus on improvement, not to criticize. Outline the process you will follow to carry out your role as coach.

It is your responsibility to assure your salespeople that coaching is a positive exercise; that you are taking this time to help them become the best they can be. The way you introduce coaching will have a great impact on the value of the first coaching calls. They need to understand that this is not a "tear down" session, but an opportunity to build.

Explain that you will be working together toward a mutual, measurable goal and that this will be an ongoing process.

Select The Fleet

Your salesperson may be tempted to take you to visit a fleet with which he/she already has a great relationship. While you should visit such fleets to thank them for their business and to keep in touch with good customers, such a call is likely to turn out to be a social visit.

Conquest Account calls are the best calls for coaching. It is there that you will have the most impact in coaching your salesperson to higher levels of performance.

Determine The Objective Of The Call

With your salesperson, determine the objective of the sales call. In reviewing the objective of the call, you will need to review the buying process and the Selling Process with your salesperson. You must jointly understand the objective of the call. The salesperson must know the objective so he/she knows what activities to pursue; you must know the objective so you can observe the techniques being used and coach the salesperson about the call later.

Discuss Appropriate Strategies

Now that you know the objective, you can help your salesperson reason through appropriate strategies. This is a coaching session. Don't tell the salesperson what to do; instead, ask what his/her thoughts are. Counsel with him/her to determine the strategies and tactics he/she will use.

Discuss And Clarify Your Role

Explain that your role is to simply attend and observe the call and that you will not take the lead during the call. If you participate in the call, or lead a discussion, you cannot coach.

During The Sales Call

Your purpose' during the sales call with your salesperson is to simply observe the call. Remember the old adage that says, "Nature gave us two ears and one mouth so we would listen twice as much as we talk?" It is true in most sales situations, but especially applicable here. This is not a joint sales call. Your job is not to add to or interfere with the sales presentation.

You must resist all temptation to jump in. If the salesperson needs or requests help with this particular customer, it is your job as the sales manager to give that assistance, but then do not use this as a coaching call.

Mental note taking and neutral body language are extremely important to your role as the silent observer. The simple fact that you are the "boss" will have an impact on the call. For your coaching to produce the results you want, you will need to be able to observe your salespeople in as natural a setting as possible.

Your pre-planning time with your salesperson will help guide your expectations of this call. Watch to see whether the plan was on target or whether the salesperson missed opportunities to advance the sale. The more familiar you are with the customer, the easier your evaluation will be.

As the coach, there are three key steps for you to follow while observing a sales call:

- Note the skills being used.
- Determine the positive points.
- Determine those areas needing improvement.

Note The Skills Being Used

As the coach, you will be observing the face-to-face sales call. Your presence may make your salesperson and/or the customer nervous. While you are "noting" the skills, do not jot notes! Instead, make a mental observation of those points you wish to cover after the meeting.

Be careful to keep your attitude neutral at all times. Any negative body language or facial expressions you make will be distracting to both your salesperson and the customer. This step is critical to your effectiveness as a coach.

It is also important to remember that you are simply an observer. You must resist the natural urge to "jump in" and "rescue" the call. If you interfere with your salesperson, you may never know if he/she had the skill necessary to salvage the situation. But more importantly, you may jeopardize the long-term relationship developed with the customer.

Determine The Positive Points

Positive skill use does not mean a "perfectly executed" sales call. Notice the rapport the salesperson establishes with the prospect. Notice whether the salesperson has credibility with the prospect. Watch for the ways in which the salesperson asks questions or speaks to the prospect.

Even in those cases where things go awry, look for a skill improvement or perhaps the use of a new technique. It is important to seek several positive points to review later, even in those situations where you feel as if you are really stretching to make the point.

Determine Those Areas Needing Improvement

Be careful! You don't want to discourage your salesperson by finding too many areas that need improvement. As you are making your mental notes, select only one or two areas that need the most improvement.

Be careful to avoid making any facial expressions or other outward indications that convey disapproval. The customer and/or the salesperson will detect your concern and it may interfere with the purpose of the call.

After The Sales Call

The review time after the sales call will include the following elements:

- Evaluate the call.
- Give feedback.
- Develop a specific action plan.

Evaluate The Call

This step is based upon the objectives you discussed during your planning session. Once again, your role is to listen. The primary goal here is to involve the salesperson in the evaluation process.

1. Ask where the prospect is in his/her buying process.
2. Ask the salesperson how they think the call went.

3. Ask what they think might have been improved.
4. Ask which areas were "stumbling blocks."

You will be asking non-judgmental questions to help focus the evaluation on specifics. It is important that you withhold any comments until your salesperson has discussed the call. Once he/she has given a self-appraisal, then you will add your comments. Be sure to have the salesperson concentrate on specifics.

Give Feedback

After the salesperson has given his/her evaluation of the call and his/her performance, it's your turn.

Begin with the positive points. Congratulate the salesperson on those areas where the call followed the plan. Tell him/her which items were particularly effective in this presentation. Be specific.

If you agree with the salesperson about the areas where he/she did poorly, tell him/her so. Instead of criticizing, use this as a learning opportunity. Ask what he/she might have done instead. Probe to help the salesperson to self-identify what might have been more effective.

Develop A Specific Action Plan

Now that you have both agreed on what went right and what went wrong, you and your salesperson should agree on two types of action steps:

- What to do with the fleet
- What skills the salesperson needs to work on

Every sales call should advance the sale. If this call was successful, the next step needs to be planned and agreed upon. Offer your support where needed and provide encouragement for the salesperson to continue the process. If the call went poorly, discuss what the salesperson might do next with the fleet. Arrive at a plan and offer your support and encouragement.

Now that you've identified the salesperson's strengths and areas for improvement, discuss how the salesperson can acquire the required skills. Support and encourage the salesperson in his/her efforts to improve.

Feedback

There are two types of feedback: positive feedback and negative feedback. Each has a place, a purpose and a result. Negative feedback should only be used to stop an undesired behavior. Before you provide the feedback, make sure the behavior is important, not a nitpicky behavior that bothers only you. Negative feedback will not create desired improvement; it should only be used to stop undesirable behavior. Negative feedback alone will get you very little in the way of productive improvement.

Positive feedback reinforces positive behavior and makes it a habit. Positive feedback is your most important tool in developing the type of professional sales force you want.

Positive feedback should be provided to any salesperson who is doing something you don't want them to quit doing. Without positive feedback, they may subconsciously come to believe that what they are doing is not important to you, so they quit doing it.

Provide positive feedback for:

- Continuing Performance. Suppose you have a salesperson who isn't a superstar, but who brings in good business regularly. Give him or her positive feedback. You want him/her to continue to bring in the business, don't you? Positive feedback will help your average performer improve. Before long, you may have a star performer.
- Improved Performance. Suppose you have a salesperson who is below average but who shows improvement. Provide positive feedback. It can work wonders in motivating the salesperson to ever greater levels of achievement.
- Outstanding Performance. When one of your people does an outstanding job, provide positive reinforcement. Tell them in front of other salespeople. Let everyone in the company know how well the salesperson performed. Encourage the salesperson to do it again and challenge him or her to even higher levels of achievement.

Feedback should be:

- SOON
- SPECIFIC
- SINCERE

Whether negative or positive, feedback should be sincere, it should be given as soon after an incident as possible, and it should include specifics about what you liked or didn't like.

Coaching Skills And Tools

Coaching is not easy. Things that are truly valuable seldom are. The rewards from the coaching process are great. Perhaps the greatest reward is watching your people develop and grow in their abilities. You can take great satisfaction from their successes. Coaching your people to greater levels of performance will be one of the most rewarding things you can do in your entire career.

To be a successful coach, you must care deeply about your people and devote the time necessary to help them succeed.

When. you coach successfully, everybody wins: your salespeople, your company, your customers and you.

14. Managing Inventory

Back in the fifth chapter we discussed the Department Critical Variables. One of those variables was managing the company assets. Your primary physical assets are the equipment inventory.

Generally you have new inventory and used inventory. Depending on your industry you might need to plan showroom displays or how to promote used units visually. For most industries you order your inventory from your OEM supplier and it may (or may not) arrive when you expect it. Some industries have large seasonal orders and other industries are just monthly activities. Your job as manager of this asset is to maintain the sales volume while keeping the inventory as low as possible. **Remember inventory is trapped cash!**

If you're the sales manager, you are beginning to understand that you have many responsibilities: Revenue, Profits, Expenses Control, Customer Satisfaction, Compensation Design and Managing the Assets (Inventory). Depending on the industry you are in there may be high or low inventory turns, but in no industry we know of are there no turns. The investment the owners make in inventory is for the purpose of making money, having equipment to show and sell immediately and to demonstrate the latest features of the product.

Your responsibility is to manage this inventory to obtain the most value out of it. Sometimes this is to have almost no inventory so that you turn the small amount of investment quickly. Usually this is in product lines that have few distinguishing differences from one model to another or so many differences that you could never stock or illustrate all of the custom options. Whatever side you might be on, you should be analyzing the inventory to make sure that it is selling, turning and not being shoved in a corner and gathering dust.

Here are a few steps to consider in managing your inventory;

1. Inventory Assessment and Optimization

Regularly assess the inventory to ensure it aligns with market demand and customer needs.

Analyze sales trends and customer feedback to adjust the inventory mix, balancing new and used equipment effectively.

Implement inventory optimization techniques to minimize carrying costs while maximizing availability and variety.

Based on your industry, manufacturer or computer system each of you could have different approaches to this, but the obvious issue is to provide the most available options to customers while minimizing the investment of cash into your inventory. I have see some manufacturers that provide multiple years of history of purchasing to aid the dealer in making advanced purchasing decisions before a seasonal requirement. Other suppliers leave the sales and purchasing analysis to the dealer and have minimal input to the process. Finally , some manufacturers will be expecting you to purchase a range of products that you might not see market demand for. This is all part of your challenge.

2. Effective Pricing Strategy

Develop a dynamic pricing strategy for new and used equipment, considering factors like market trends, equipment condition, and depreciation.

Regularly review and adjust prices based on competitive analysis and internal cost structures.

Employ pricing models that attract customers while ensuring a reasonable profit margin.

Pricing strategy might not immediately feel like inventory control, but if your prices on certain products is too high they will sit in inventory and never sell. Generally this is obvious on the new equipment units, but is much more challenging when dealing with used units. Used units will vary in price based on age, number of hours on the engine, previous operating environment, historical maintenance and your reconditioning.

You also have some control of setting pricing for used equipment with possibly a three tiered pricing structure:

1. Used Units "As-Is," where you have invested no reconditioning expense.
2. Touch up work, from brakes to engine tune-up, and possibly a 30 dealership warranty.
3. Extensive reconditioning, including engine work, brakes, hydraulics, etc. and possibly a level of repainting, which you then add a 90 day dealership warranty to.

Obviously, the three levels of used equipment reconditioning would have different price points even if the three units were exactly the same. But the focus here is that you can change the price point, the profit margin and the marketability of the used units, it is not a customer controlled situation.

3. Quality Control and Equipment Maintenance

Implement stringent quality control checks for both new and used equipment to maintain high standards.

Schedule regular maintenance and repairs for used equipment to enhance its value and prolong its usability.

Train staff in effective maintenance practices and the importance of maintaining equipment in sale-ready condition.

What are your standards for new equipment preparation. When the equipment is delivered from your OEM supplier, what else does your dealership expect needs to be done before it is available for deliver to a customer? You should have this documented and ensure that it is followed. This could be a checklist that the service department uses and then signs off on before returning it to the sales department for customer delivery or to be placed in inventory.

In many dealerships, this standard checklist of procedures has been priced by the service department, discussed with the sales manager and is fixed as a flat rate add on price to the basic cost of the unit. Salespeople therefore know what is included and can sell those features to the customer.

Also, if an inventory item has been in the inventory for an extended period you might have procedures established to make sure it is still in good running and sales condition.

4. Inventory Turnover and Liquidation Strategies

Monitor inventory turnover rates to identify slow-moving items and devise strategies to increase their turnover.

Develop liquidation strategies for outdated or excess stock, such as discounts, trade-ins, or auctions.

Balance the need for a diverse inventory with the risks of overstocking, especially for models with lower demand.

Some sales managers adjust the commission rate on older or slow moving units. Other sales managers understand the possibility of trading certain units with neighboring dealers who might have a different customer population. What sells in one territory might not sell well in another territory.

Some people (and that goes from dealer principals to service technicians) have difficulty getting rid of an item that has been purchased and is not moving. But there are times that the handling cost, carrying cost, interest, and insurance costs will out weigh any loss in the price of selling the unit at a loss. It has been calculated that the "carrying cost" of inventory can range from 10-25% of the investment each year. So a Unit that was purchased for $10,000, which could bring a profit of $2,000, but is now a year old might be more valuable to sell at $8,000 and reinvest that money back into better moving inventory.

If you have obsolete inventory that has not moved in years, it will be painful to make this initial change, but once you start doing this every 6-12 months, the number of units that need attention will be less and easier to accept the adjustment.

In fact, would you consider an aging of your inventory value like you see accounts receivable aged? Think of this chart below:

Aging	Current	Over 6 Months	Over 12 Months	Over 24 Months
% of Dollar Value	70.0%	25.0%	5.0%	0.0%

Based on original date the equipment was added to your inventory, how will your equipment inventory rate against this chart?

5. Technological Integration and Data Analysis

Utilize inventory management software to track stock levels, sales patterns, and customer preferences efficiently.

Analyze data collected from sales and customer interactions to forecast future inventory needs accurately.

Invest in technology that streamlines inventory management processes, reducing manual errors and saving time.

There are systems today with bar code, QR code and RFID that can assist in identifying equipment locations. Even GPS tracking for equipment that gets moved from the dealer's lot to customers locations for demonstration or sales presentations. You're no longer chained to paper and pencil, or manual computer input for transactions. Smartphones and mobile devices provide considerable technical options for each dealer, almost regardless of size.

6. Customer-Centric Inventory Approach

Understand customer preferences and market needs to tailor the inventory accordingly.

Engage with customers through feedback and surveys to gain insights into their equipment needs and preferences.

Use customer-centric approaches to inventory management, ensuring the availability of equipment that meets the specific demands of your target market.

Back n the chapter about CRMs (Customer Relationship Managers) we mentioned the idea of tracking the equipment owned by customers and prospects. With good information like this you can also utilize that to determine some of your inventory mix. If you don't have the unit available some customers just move on to your competitor.

Inventory Turn Over & Planning

Some dealerships have very sophisticated computer systems which track the models and details of equipment sales to determine how much "stock" you should have in the warehouse or on the floor. In other companies this is done in a spreadsheet or by hand. In general we expect you to track the history of equipment units, keeping in mind what was sold out of stock and what was ordered specifically for a customer or job. Then determining what needs to be actually in the dealership to handle spontaneous sales, coverage of delivery problems and substitution of any problems which occur in sales. (We might ask why you would have "spontaneous sales" if your salespeople are covering all the accounts and doing annual business plans for each account... but then we expect you already understand the sarcasm in that question.)

In good purchasing procedures for the sales department we would never expect you to have any equipment over one year old. This would indicate that you made a mistake in your determination of "stock" inventory or ordered a unit for a customer incorrectly and could not make an adjustment.

Sometimes the "older than one year" problem comes up with units you accepted in trade for new equipment. Possibly you over valued the trade-in or just did not have very good plan for who was going to purchase the used equipment.

While we don't have time to write an entire book on the used equipment, trade-ins, rental disposal process; there are a couple points that should be made to sales managers who want to really manage their inventory well.

The first point is ask, insist and train salespeople that when they are going to accept a trade-in unit that it is their responsibility to KNOW who will purchase it before you accept the trade-in. In this procedure the salesperson needs to look at the unit, identify a customer or prospect who will be interested and show you that they have already talked to this prospect for the equipment and in some cases actually have signed a quotation to purchase it if it becomes available. In this method you will have almost no used equipment in your inventory. That is good use of the inventory investment in making sales.

Sometimes you are promoted and you inherit extra (sometimes old) inventory. What can you do about the extra or excess inventory? First organize it, get specific detail about what it is, where it is, conditions and values. Then start doing a historical search of your previous company's sales and find what customers 3, 4 or 5 years ago purchased that type of equipment and might be ready to replace it now with this good unit you have in stock. Coach the salespeople about how to sell this replacement unit to the very targeted accounts, and what the pricing will be, whether you will accept trade-ins when selling these units, and what range of pricing you will allow them to use to make the sale.

Old equipment sitting in the warehouse or in the yard is not a good use of money. Sometimes you have to make hard decisions to sell the units at auction or to wholesalers. When selling to wholesalers, you sometimes improve the value of the sale when you group equipment into packages instead of letting the wholesaler price each unit they are buying.

The Position of Sales in Inventory Levels

It has been our experience working with over 400 dealers a year in 10 different industries that the good salespeople do not clutter the inventory of the dealership with their mistakes. They know their accounts, what sells, who buys, what certain accounts like, etc. They work a very tight arrangement of what they order in, what they need in inventory and what they bring in on trade they usually know how to liquidate. If you find a strong salesperson who is not doing this, we frequently find a dealership or previous history of their employment where the dealership (read sales manager) did not train them well and make them responsible for this control.

It is partly your direction and insistence of policy and procedure that will make a good sales team. When you say this is how things will be, the salespeople believe you if they see you holding to your direction and holding them accountable. Eventually they learn that you expect results from them, and you support them in getting results and you recognize their success when it occurs. Management creates the game and writes the rules and enforces the rules. If all of that happens together, they will work with it. IF it doesn't work together, they will find out how to manipulate the rules, the game or the enforcement.

15. Action Worksheets

Account Assignment Worksheet

Sales Rep Name: -______________________

Account Segment	**Number of Accounts**	**Call Frequency**	**Annual Calls Per Account**	**Total Annual Calls (Number X Annual Calls)**
'A' Accounts				
High Priority				
Medium Priority				
Low Priority				
'B' Accounts				
High Priority				
Medium Priority				
Low Priority				
'C' Accounts				
High Priority				
Medium Priority				
Low Priority				
'D' Accounts				
High Priority				
Medium Priority				
Low Priority				
Totals				**800**

Call Frequency Worksheet

Account Segment	Number of Accounts	Call Frequency	Annual Calls Per Account	Total Annual Calls (Number X Annual Calls)
'A' Accounts				
High Priority				
Medium Priority				
Low Priority				
'B' Accounts				
High Priority				
Medium Priority				
Low Priority				
'C' Accounts				
High Priority				
Medium Priority				
Low Priority				
'D' Accounts				
High Priority				
Medium Priority				
Low Priority				
Totals				

Sales Department Compensation Design Worksheet

Description	Financial Model Benchmarks	Model Performance	Actual Performance	Gap From Model Performance
Total Revenue Generated				
Total Gross Profit				
Base Salary				
Commission				
Incentives				
Taxes				
Medical Coverage				
Retirement/401k Matching				
Total Annual Compensation				
Cell Phone Allowance				
Other Sales Expense Allowance				
Car/Truck Allowance				
Total Expense per Sales Person				

Competition Worksheet

Company	Ownership	Brands	Equipment Sales Performance	Aftermarket Sales Performance	Financial Performance	Customer Satisfaction	Visibility
Competition **A**							
Competition **B**							
Competition **C**							
Competition **D**							
Your Company							

Attach Geographic Maps of Each Company's Area of Responsibility by Brand.
Attach Individual Sheets of SWOT (Strength, Weakness, Opportunities & Threats

Sales Department Financial Worksheet

Description	Financial Model Benchmarks	Model Performance	Actual Performance	Gap From Model Performance
Sales				
Cost of Goods				
Gross Profit	**100.0%**			
Management Wages	7.0%			
Sale People Wages	30.0%			
Clerical Wages	3.0%			
Other Wages	0.0%			
Taxes & Benefits	10.0%			
Total Personnel	**50.0%**			
Operating Expenses	25.0%			
Occupancy	10.0%			
Total Expenses	**85.0%**			
Department Net Profit	**15.0%**			

Quotation Log Worksheet

Quote #	Customer Name	Slsp	Equipment Quoted	Type of Quote	Amount

Won / Lost	Competition	Status	Reason Won/Lost	Date of Last Update	

Total Units Sold / Total Quoted Units = Close Rate

Salesperson Performance Worksheet

Sales Person Rank	Revenue Level in Dollars	Gross Profit Dollars	Gross Profit %	Salesperson Compensation	Compensation as Percentage of GP $	Years of Experience	Number of Accounts
A Level							
B Level							
C Level							
D Level							
Average							

Sales Rep Productivity Expectations Worksheet

Rep Name or Initials	Sales Rep Level (A, B or C)	Revenue Expectation	GP Expectation	Calls per Day	Calls per Year

Sales Manager Weekly Worksheet

Monday	Tuesday	Wednesday	Thursday	Friday	Saturday
Ride with Slsp # 1	Ride with Slsp # 2	Major Acct Calls	Ride with Slsp # 3	Meet with Slsp # 1	
				Meet with Slsp # 2	
					Sunday
		Major Acct Calls			
				Meet with Slsp # 3	

Salesperson Conference Worksheet

Agenda Items	Acct #1 [Name]	Acct #2 [Name]	Acct #3 [Name]	Activities and Other Accounts	
Acct Segment				Total Open Quotes	
Number of Units Owned				Number of Calls Last Week	
Date Last Purchased				Number of Calls Scheduled This Week	
Brand Preferences				Other Managers You Need for Calls	
Buying Phase					
Key Decision Makers					
Sales Strategy					
Competition				Acct Disputes You Are Working On	
Expected Purchase Date					
Unit Quantities					

Preparing the Sales Message to Target Accounts

Customer Phase	Describe the Package of Value	Customer / Cost Data Required	Analyses to be Performed
I *(Wants premium product and will pay premium price)*			
II *(Buys on price alone)*			
III *(Focusing on cost of ownership cycle)*			
IV *(Focus on cost of process; looking to outsource process)*			

Index

About The Author

George Keen - Principal Consultant

George Keen is a principal consultant and a renowned authority in operational excellence and strategic execution across the construction, materials handling, and agricultural equipment industries. His career is distinguished by an unwavering dedication to operational enhancements, training initiatives, and strategic development, making him an invaluable asset to businesses striving for the pinnacle of industry leadership.

At the heart of George's expertise lies a keen focus on optimizing equipment sales, account management, and the operational dynamics of service, parts, and rental divisions. His innovative approach to seminar delivery has established new benchmarks for industry best practices. Furthermore, George is adept at devising performance management systems, compensation structures, incentive programs, and strategies for enhancing productivity and business turnaround.

George's foray into consultancy is underpinned by a rich tapestry of experience that spans managing retail hardware and dedicating a decade to software development within the lift truck sector. A pioneer in marrying technology with business operations, he played a pivotal role in the early adoption of computer systems for accounting and financial management during the digital transformation era of the 1960s and 1970s.

His tenure as a consultant is marked by a forward-thinking approach to training and development, particularly through the deployment of internet-based training programs. These initiatives have disseminated industry knowledge and trends and significantly elevated employee performance and operational efficiency across North America, Europe, and Latin America.

George's practical insights also stem from his tenures in a John Deere Agricultural dealership and a Caterpillar forklift dealership, which gave him a holistic understanding of dealership operations and customer service excellence.

In response to the evolving industry landscape, particularly the challenges posed by the pandemic, George launched Wise Wolf Consulting, LLC. This venture is a testament to his unwavering commitment to supporting equipment dealers across North America in achieving operational excellence, adaptability, and sustained growth, which are crucial in these times.

George Keen's legacy is one of innovation, leadership, and an unrelenting pursuit of excellence, dedicated to propelling the equipment industry forward through his comprehensive expertise and visionary perspective.

Testimonials from esteemed colleagues and clients underscore George's profound impact on individuals and businesses alike. Known for his resourcefulness, innovative thinking, and unparalleled service orientation, George possesses a unique insight into industry dynamics and culture. His mentorship and ethical standards have shaped careers, driven client success, and solidified his status as a trusted business partner and friend.

Milton Keynes UK
Ingram Content Group UK Ltd.
UKHW051103280324
440302UK00002B/7